Building Identity

A TRAINING PROGRAMME

Kate Cairns and Eileen Fursland

This training programme comprises one-day courses on:

- **Identity and child development**
- **Life story work**
- **Sibling relationships**
- **Contact**

AKAMAS

BAAF
ADOPTION & FOSTERING

Published by
British Association for Adoption & Fostering
(BAAF)
Saffron House
6–10 Kirby Street
London EC1N 8TS

www.baaf.org.uk

Charity registration 275689 (England and Wales)
and SC039337 (Scotland)

© Akamas, 2008

British Library Cataloguing in Publication Data

A catalogue record for this book is available from the British Library

ISBN 978 1 905664 43 6

Project management by Jo Francis, BAAF
Designed by Andrew Haig & Associates
Typeset by Avon DataSet Ltd, Bidford on Avon
Printed in Great Britain by the Lavenham Press

Trade distribution by Turnaround Publisher Services, Unit 3,
Olympia Trading Estate, Coburg Road, London N22 6TZ

BAAF is the leading UK-wide membership organisation for
all those concerned with adoption, fostering and child care issues.

Contents

Notes about the authors

Kate Cairns is a social worker and social work teacher. With her partner, Brian, and their three birth children, she provided permanence for a group of 12 looked after children, all of whom are now adult. She and Brian recently founded Akamas, a training organisation which provides online training for foster carers – www.akamas.co.uk. Kate is also the author of *Attachment, Trauma and Resilience: Therapeutic caring for children*, *Learn the Child: Helping looked after children to learn* (with Chris Stanway), *Trauma and Recovery: A training programme* (with Eileen Fursland), *Safer Caring: A training programme* (with Eileen Fursland), and *Transitions and Endings: A training programme* (with Eileen Fursland), all published by BAAF.

Eileen Fursland is a professional freelance writer. She has written a number of books and feature stories for magazines, amongst them *Preparing to Adopt: A training pack for preparation groups* for BAAF (alongside a BAAF working party), *A Guide for Medical Advisers: Advocating, promoting and protecting the health of looked after children in Scotland* (with Ian Millar), *Trauma and Recovery: A training programme* (with Kate Cairns), *Safer Caring: A training programme* (with Kate Cairns), *Transitions and Endings: A training programme* (with Kate Cairns) and a series of six booklets on caring for unaccompanied asylum-seeking children and young people, all published by BAAF.

Also in this series

Trauma and Recovery: A training programme, by Kate Cairns and Eileen Fursland

This course is designed to enable foster carers and adoptive parents to help children adapt to developmental impairments caused by trauma and to build their resilience.

Safer Caring: A training programme, by Kate Cairns and Eileen Fursland

This course aims to give foster carers the knowledge they need to prevent, recognise and get the right treatment for secondary traumatic stress disorders, to access and manage risk and to work as part of a team to provide safer caring.

Transitions and Endings: A training programme, by Kate Cairns and Eileen Fursland

This course is designed to enable foster carers and adoptive parents to help children adjust to transitions, including moving placement, and also to help carers themselves to face change and loss in a managed and constructive way.

Introduction

What this course will do

This training programme has been designed to help social workers, foster carers, adoptive families and staff in residential homes to understand more about how to help traumatised children to form a strong and positive identity. It also looks at life story work; sibling relationships; and contact between traumatised children and members of their birth family.

Most foster carers and prospective adoptive parents will attend a general preparation course, during which they will learn something about these issues, but *Building Identity* goes into much more detail than is possible in a general course.

Most children separated from their birth relatives will have suffered distortions and disruptions in the attachment process, with long-term damage to their sense of identity. They need help to overcome this if they are to grow up to be comfortable in their own skin. Understanding how we form our sense of identity – identifying with some people and groups, and differentiating ourselves from others – gives carers insight into why this might be difficult for a child whose early attachment experiences were disrupted.

This course also looks at the complexity of relationships between siblings and the question of whether they should be cared for together or apart; the contribution of informal and formal life story work to children's wellbeing; and managing risk where there is to be contact with birth relatives.

Why carers need this course

Babies' early interactions with caregivers shape their sense of self and their developing personality. Where there is neglect, rejection or abuse, overwhelming stress damages the baby's developing brain and affects physical, emotional, social and cognitive development in countless ways. Distortions and disruptions in early attachment relationships have far-reaching effects on the way children see themselves and relate to other people.

Looking after children who have suffered in this way and making decisions about their lives is a challenging task. Carers and social workers need to be able to help children and young people to make sense of their troubled histories. To do this, they need the best possible training and support.

This course explains how, with knowledge, understanding and skill from everyone involved, it is possible for the child to grow up into an individual with a positive sense of who he or she is and where he or she has come from, someone who is tolerant of, and can celebrate, "difference" in themselves and others.

How to use these training materials

This training programme works best with groups of between 8 and 20 participants. It is made up of four courses covering various aspects of **identity and contact**. The material in this pack contains PowerPoint presentations for each of the four courses, and there are two sessions per course.

Identity and child development: celebrating diversity in the care of traumatised children

- Session A: Identity, diversity and infant attachment
- Session B: Enabling traumatised children to form a strong sense of identity and to celebrate diversity

Life story work: enabling children to make sense of their lives

- Session A: Child development and the creation of narrative
- Session B: Enabling traumatised children to form a strong and positive personal narrative

Family ties: working with issues in the care of siblings

- Session A: The complexity of sibling relationships
- Session B: Assessment and planning

Contact: issues of identity and stability

- Session A: Understanding the complexity of contact
- Session B: Making child-centred contact plans

The training can be delivered flexibly in several different ways, depending on what works best for the agency and participants. It could be given:

- as four linked courses (either on consecutive days or separated by days or weeks)
- as a course of two days or more, incorporating the first course, **Identity and child development**, plus any of the other courses, depending on the particular needs of the agency's clients.
- as a series of eight evening sessions
- as individual stand-alone courses

The training has been designed so that the timing can be flexible. Each course lasts around three hours, although this can vary either way. If the agency wants the trainer to go into the subjects in more depth, there is the option to spend longer on discussion and training exercises. A single session could be delivered in an evening. Alternatively it could be given in one day, allowing more time for discussion and training exercises. This could start at 10am and end at 3.15pm, which allows time for a coffee break and a lunch break, finishing in time to allow participants to collect children from school. With an earlier start and a later finish, two sessions could be combined in one day of training if necessary.

Participants often learn a great deal from hearing about other people's experiences. This is why the courses include a number of training exercises in which participants work in small groups, sharing their ideas and thoughts, often feeding back the key points to the rest of the group. These training exercises, discussions and sharing experiences are valuable elements of the learning, so should be included if at all possible. But if time is short, trainers can use their discretion and keep the training exercises brief or even omit some of them. Coffee breaks or the lunch break can also be used as discussion times.

What this pack includes

- a **CD-ROM** containing **PowerPoint presentations** and a set of **handouts**. The handouts may be printed out and photocopied for distribution to participants attending the course; they may not be used for other purposes unless permission is sought.

- this **book**, which contains the following:
  - reproductions of the PowerPoint slide presentations for each of the four courses (each presentation includes the learning outcomes for that course);
  - supplementary material to help the trainer to comment further on the points made on the slides;
  - suggested training exercises, usually for small group work, to encourage participants to share their thoughts, ideas and experiences and to encourage reflection and learning;
  - suggested questions which the trainer can raise with the group, briefly and informally, at certain points in the presentation.

What you will need

- A flipchart and marker pens

- A laptop computer with CD-ROM drive and PowerPoint

- A screen for displaying PowerPoint slides

- Pens, pencils and coloured crayons for participants to use

Venue

Ideally, this course should be held in a venue that is well-heated, well-lit, comfortable and welcoming. You will need adequate seating for participants and access to tables will be helpful. You will probably want somewhere that provides refreshments or has provision for making drinks. If you are presenting this course in full-day sessions, you will also need somewhere which provides lunch or opportunities for participants to buy lunch, or bring lunch with them to eat in the venue. You will need to think about whether your venue is easily accessible to carers. Is it on good transport routes? Is there disabled access? Parking? Is there a crèche?

Evaluation

On the CD-ROM, an evaluation form is provided for participants to complete and return. This is important for the course leaders, your organisation and for the carers themselves. Evaluation allows the service users to voice their opinions of the training and to contribute to improvements in its provision, and it provides you and your organisation with invaluable feedback about the impact and effectiveness of what you do.

How to run training groups

Preparation

The course can be delivered by a single trainer, ideally someone with experience in the area of fostering or adoption. Agencies should ensure that course leaders:

- have the necessary training skills;

- have an understanding of adult learning principles;

- are familiar with the course content and are confident in delivering this;

- are committed to anti-discriminatory practice.

It would help trainers a great deal in delivering this course if they have read *Attachment, Trauma and Resilience: Therapeutic caring for children*, by Kate Cairns (BAAF, 2002).

Dealing with difficult issues

This course will invite and expect participants to reflect on their own experience as well as the experience of traumatised children. As a trainer, you need to emphasise the value of everyone's prior life experience, whether they are experienced carers or new to the role.

Many participants will have looked after children to whom they became attached. Some will have had difficulties because of the child's distorted sense of identity or sibling relationships, or have been disturbed or angered by the child's experiences of contact with birth relatives. Be prepared for some strong and painful emotions.

As a trainer, you will need to be aware of all these possibilities and be prepared to help acknowledge and deal with the feelings that emerge.

Reflective discussion and training exercises

Asking participants about their own views and experiences encourages open discussion, shows them how much they already know and allows them to learn from each other. However, trainers should feel free to include different training exercises or bring up other points for discussion if they feel these would work better with their particular group of participants.

Group dynamics

In any group of people, there will be some who say a lot and some who say very little; some who are dominant and appear to have all the answers, and others who seem to have little confidence in the value of their own views and experiences.

Some people feel uncomfortable with the material and individuals have different ways of dealing with this. While there is a place for humour even on a course like this, you may find your group contains someone who feels the need to be "the life and soul of the party". Experience teaches teachers and trainers ways in which they can diplomatically handle participants who never seem to stop talking or never miss the opportunity to crack a joke.

Some participants may be very experienced in fostering traumatised children; others may feel almost as though they have no right to be on the course because they are still waiting for a child to be placed with them. Some may be managing well with the child or young person placed with them; others will be struggling and feeling inadequate. Every trainer has his or her own teaching style, but whatever your individual style, it is your responsibility to put people at their ease, encourage everyone to make a contribution and help the group "gel". You need to be sensitive to the way the individuals within the group are feeling. If necessary, you may have to tactfully encourage this sensitivity among certain participants in the group as well.

Be aware of what is going on in the small groups as they work together. If one or two groups are being dominated by particular individuals or you can see personalities clashing, mix up the groups in different ways. People learn in different ways, so it is not necessary for everyone to speak out the whole time in order to get value from the course – but do make sure that every participant has the space and opportunity to speak and ask questions if they want to. Sometimes one participant gets "hung up" on a particular issue or question and doesn't want to let it drop. 'Let's talk more about this later over coffee – we have a lot to fit in and I think we need to move on now' is one way to handle this.

Diversity issues

It is your responsibility to ensure that the course is accessible to everyone and that all participants – whatever their ethnic background, sexuality or educational level – feel equally valued, respected and able to contribute. As a trainer, you need to be sensitive to the composition of the group and consider how you will include and address the needs of participants who are from minority ethnic groups, who have a disability, who are single or gay or lesbian.

If any participants have disabilities, check the accessibility of the building and the layout of the room and if necessary, make sure a parking space will be available for them close to the building. Asking participants in advance about any disabilities will forewarn you about the need for a British Sign Language interpreter or the need to provide handouts in a larger type size, for instance.

When setting dates for training, be careful not to clash with any religious holidays.

The course may be targeted at a particular ethnic group – in which case you may of course deliver the course in the appropriate language. In other cases, where necessary, consider the need for interpreters to work alongside the trainer.

When setting ground rules at the start of the course, make it clear to all the participants that you will challenge any discriminatory attitudes or remarks. You may wish to tackle the issues head-on, by stating that your agency values gay and lesbian people who can offer care and stability to children, just as much as it values heterosexual people – either single people or couples – who can do the same.

First things first

Every time you give the course to a new group or to the same group in a different venue:

- Start by introducing yourself.

- Explain the arrangements for the day: what time and where you will be having refreshments and lunch, and what time the course will finish.

- Ask if anyone will need to leave before the end of the course.

- Tell participants where the toilets are and what to do if the fire alarm sounds.

- Make sure everyone can see you (and the screen) and hear you.

- Make sure they are comfortable with the room temperature.

- Ask them to turn their mobile phones to "silent".

- Talk about issues such as confidentiality and the sensitivity of the subject matter.

- Give participants a handout of the slide presentation so they do not need to write everything down.

How this course came about

I am a social worker and social work teacher. My partner Brian and I, along with our three birth children, fostered 12 children over a 25-year period. Between 1975 and 2000, in our large family home in rural Gloucestershire, which was provided by a charitable trust, we offered permanence to the children as part of our family group. The children joined the family at various stages of their childhood, ranging in age from 4 to 15. The children had all experienced overwhelming stress in early life. Between them they displayed all the rage and fear, grief and disturbed, destructive and self-destructive behaviour that so often follow attachment difficulties, loss, abuse and trauma.

The knowledge and experience that we gained as we responded to the children's difficulties and helped promote their recovery forms the foundation of this training material. We built on our experience of the realities of family life with traumatised children by drawing on knowledge and ideas absorbed from theory and research. We developed a model which explains how stress damages the brain – a model which also provides for healing and recovery. We showed that, in the right conditions and with the right help, children can learn to adapt to the impairments and difficulties that are the legacy of overwhelming stress. A fulfilled and happy life need not be beyond their reach.

All of our foster children are now grown up. Almost all remain in contact with us and most are in regular and frequent contact.

Brian and I went on to form a company, Akamas Training, to share our knowledge and experience with foster carers, social workers and other professionals working in the field. Akamas provides online training for social workers, foster carers and others who work with traumatised children. It provides a route to two qualifications in foster care, a BTEC Advanced Certificate and a BTEC Professional Certificate – delivered and assessed online. Akamas also runs one-day training courses.

BAAF wanted to make this valuable training more widely available to foster carers and social workers across the UK. So, working in partnership, BAAF and Akamas have adapted the online learning material into courses that agencies themselves can deliver, in a flexible way, to meet the training needs of their foster carers, prospective adoptive parents and social workers. Such training can stand alone, or can complement the online BTEC qualifications.

Kate Cairns
March 2008

1 Identity and child development

Identity, diversity and infant attachment

Setting the scene

This is the first session of the course, so welcome the participants, introduce yourself and put them at their ease.

Explain what they can expect from the course – that there will be some direct input from you, in terms of your presentation, but that they also have a lot to contribute from their own knowledge and experience. Explain that they will not simply be sitting and listening to you – they will be actively involved in discussion and group exercises, coming up with their own thoughts, ideas and suggestions.

Also briefly explain the context to the learning material and how it came to be developed, referring to Kate Cairns' experience and expertise (as detailed in the introductory material).

This course deals with formative influences in childhood and their effect on children's sense of identity; it also covers issues such as discrimination on the grounds of race, ethnicity, sexual orientation and so on. These are subjects that can touch on difficult and sometimes painful areas of people's experience. Everyone needs to be sensitive to the fact that some participants may have direct personal experience of discrimination and oppression. Reassure people that they will not be asked to disclose or discuss anything that they would rather keep to themselves.

Introduction

Ask participants to introduce themselves to the rest of the group. If this is the start of a longer course, for instance, running over two or three days, you might want to have more extended introductions, asking the participants to talk about why they are here and what they hope to gain from the course.

Establish ground rules

Invite participants to suggest some rules for how they should behave on the training course. Write these suggestions on a flip chart and leave them on display for the rest of the course. The points might include, for instance:

- Turn off mobile phones or at least put them on "silent" mode.

- Keep confidential everything that people share within the group about their or their children's experiences.

- Respect difference – this is a key message of the course. Participants will also come from a variety of backgrounds and have a range of perspectives. Everyone should respect these differences.

- Don't be afraid to ask questions.

- If anyone disagrees with what someone else has said, they should challenge the statement but respect the person.

- Listen to others as well as talking about your own views and experiences.

Provide the handout

Give participants a handout of the slide presentation so that they do not need to write everything down and, if they wish, they can make notes on their handout.

The Presentation

SLIDE 1

Identity and child development: celebrating diversity in the care of traumatised children

Most children in our society grow up knowing they are loved and cherished. Their parents and other adults spend a lot of time and effort in keeping them safe, nurturing them, teaching them, taking pleasure in their company and celebrating their achievements. In the normal course of events they grow up with a positive sense of their own life story and a healthy degree of self-esteem.

Sadly, many children who come into the care system have had the opposite experience. Their early experiences of neglect, abuse and loss mean it is difficult for them to form a positive sense of their own identity. They may grow up with the feeling that they are worthless, stupid, a nuisance, or a commodity to be exploited.

Every child is unique. As a carer or social worker, it is pretty certain that at some stage you will work with children from a different ethnicity, culture or social background from your own, as well as children with disabilities. You may also work with young people who are gay. Some children may have been brought up by adults who reject them or belittle them on any of these grounds. Some may have experienced oppression or discrimination in wider society.

Part of your work with every child is to try to repair the damage that has been done to their sense of identity. You aim to help them not only to feel they "belong", but also to be accepting and even proud of the things that make them different from others.

SLIDE 2

Learning outcomes

- **To understand the importance of identification and differentiation**
- **To understand why the attachment process is key to the child's sense of identity**
- **To consider the effect of unmet attachment needs**
- **To consider the effect of diversity issues on identity formation**
- **To understand how to help children celebrate diversity**

This slide shows the learning outcomes for Sessions A and B, *Identity, diversity and infant attachment* and *Enabling traumatised children to form a strong sense of identity and to celebrate diversity*. Session A now begins.

SLIDE 3   Who are you?

- Jot down five words or phrases that would complete a sentence beginning *'I am . . .'* if you were talking to someone about yourself
- Try to pick out words or phrases that for you have some importance
- Discuss your list with people around you
  - Are there any bits of the list that you could easily give up or change?
  - Are there any that would be very painful to change?
  - Are there any that would be impossible to change?

Exercise: Who are you?

Give participants 15 minutes to complete this exercise.

Before you show Slide 3, set participants the first task – to pick five words or phrases that feel important to them when describing themselves. The slide shows discussion points for participants to talk about in small groups. Some participants may be reticent about discussing something personal with people they don't know, but that shouldn't be a problem as you will probably find that each group has one or two members who will happily talk about themselves for as long as they are allowed!

SLIDE 4   Identity

- **As human beings we form a sense of who we are in two ways:**
- **Identification**
  - **We identify ourselves as similar to others**
- **Differentiation**
  - **We identify ourselves as different from others**

Ask participants to look at their lists again with "identification" and "differentiation" in mind. They will realise that some of their words or phrases may indicate ways in which they identify with a group – 'I am Jewish', 'I am a Manchester United fan', 'I am a member of the Labour Party' – while others will be more to do with differentiation – 'I am the mother of a child who is deaf', 'I am a great cook', 'I am taller than anyone else I know'.

SLIDE 5   With whom do you identify yourself?

- Make a list of all the people or groups with whom you identify yourself
- Discuss your list with people around you
  - How does your relationship with this person or your membership of this group add to your sense of identity?
  - Are there any issues for you in this identification?
- What are the key points arising from this discussion?

Exercise: Identifying with others

Give participants 10 minutes to complete this exercise.

Slide 5 asks participants to focus on the ways they identify with others. They may list their family, their religion, particular racial or ethnic groups, socio-economic groups, people of a particular sexual orientation, or people who enjoy the same hobby, support the same sports team or are fans of a particular kind of music or band. Some of these groupings will be regarded as positive and people are proud to declare their allegiance to them. However, there may be other groupings – slimming clubs; divorcees; widows – which they wish they didn't have to belong to.

Ask participants to discuss the questions on the slide in their small groups.

SLIDE 6   What makes you unique?

- There is no one in the world exactly like you
- Make a list of all the things about yourself that make you feel unique, special or different
- Discuss your list with people around you
  - Was this list easier or harder to do? Or was it just the same?
  - Do you come from a family or culture that values identification, or differentiation, or both?
- What are the key points arising from this discussion?

Exercise: What makes you unique?

Give participants 10 minutes to complete this exercise.

Encourage participants to think of things about themselves that make them unique or special. They may have a particular talent or skill, for example: 'I play jazz piano'; 'I write poetry' or 'I speak fluent Russian'. It may be as simple as something unusual about their appearance: 'I have one green eye and one brown eye'. They may cite personal attributes such as patience or their ability to empathise with troubled children.

If they refer to adverse circumstances or personal difficulties, for example, 'I have a stammer',

'I have survived a bad car crash' or 'I have lost my hair' – invite them to reflect on what they have learned about coping with and transcending adverse events and why this has made them into the person they are.

Ask them to think about how much they value the things that make them unique, and discuss the questions on the slide in their small groups.

Some of the groups people identify with may at the same time differentiate them from other groups they belong to. For example, 'I am the only member of my family who is a practising Christian' or 'Among my work colleagues, I am the only one who went to university'.

SLIDE 7   Differentiation and diversity

- **Identification with others is an essential early stage in human development**
- **Such identification automatically produces membership groups**
- **If identification is overvalued, majority or powerful groups and individuals may discriminate against minority or less powerful groups and individuals**
- **If differentiation is overvalued, social cohesion may be lost and anomie results**
- **If both processes are valued, social cohesion is maintained and diversity can be tolerated, and may be welcomed and celebrated**

Some families, cultures and faiths (and even some workplaces) place a high value on "belonging" and discourage individual expression. Members of the family, culture, faith or organisation are expected to dress and behave in a certain way or to have certain beliefs and values – and anyone who does not conform or fit in is frowned on.

Ask participants to think about countries and societies in which identification has been overvalued and discrimination against certain groups has developed. Think, for instance, about Nazi Germany and the Holocaust; about the fierce clan and tribal loyalties that lead to conflict in various African countries and even genocide in the case of Rwanda. There are many countries in the world where minority political parties are not tolerated, ethnic minorities suffer discrimination and members of dissenting political or religious groups or homosexuals are persecuted.

Think about intolerance and overvalued identification closer to home and on a smaller scale: the teenage gangs in Britain's inner cities who feel justified in attacking members of other gangs; the tragic case in 2007 in which a young woman was beaten to death by a gang of other teenagers simply for being a "goth".

Problems can also occur when the emphasis on individualism is so great that there is little sense of community and many people feel that they don't "belong" anywhere.

"**Anomie**" is a word that comes from Greek (a = "without" and $nomos$ = "law") and is used to describe an individual's sense of personal alienation and a lack of purpose and ideals.

Emile Durkheim, a late 19th century sociologist, used this term when he wrote about crime and suicide. He introduced the concept of anomie as a condition that arises in certain societies when social change means that old rules and systems of values disappear and people no longer know what rules to live by. He believed the division of labour in economic life since the Industrial Revolution led to conditions in which people were more likely to experience anomie.

In his book, *The Division of Labour in Society* (1997), Durkheim proposed that when societies become more complex, work also becomes more complex. In this society, people are no longer tied to one another, they no longer feel they are working for the good of the larger community, and social bonds are impersonal. Social norms break down and, Durkheim said, individuals cannot find their place in society without clear rules to help guide them. He observed that periods of social disruption (such as economic depression) brought about greater anomie and higher rates of crime and suicide.

SLIDE 8 — Diversity issues

- Issues that may lead to majority or powerful groups oppressing or discriminating against less powerful groups or individuals
- Diversity issues may include:
  - Gender
  - Culture
  - Ethnicity
  - "Race"
  - Sexuality and sexual orientation
  - Disability
  - Age
  - And so on

When identification is overvalued in a society, discrimination and oppression can result. This can also happen, of course, with religion. Religions often provide a basis for shared values. However, when adherence to a religion is overvalued and its adherents abuse their power, it can lead to conflict, for example, the hundreds of years of conflict between Catholics and Protestants in Northern Ireland, or the persecution of Catholics and Protestants that has occurred in the UK at various times in our history.

If it is not too contentious, you could also cite the position of women in certain Muslim societies and the rigid codes they are expected to meet regarding their dress and their behaviour.

As we have seen, identifying with and differentiating ourselves from other people and groups are essential in building identity. The rest of this session looks at the process by which babies and children develop attachment and a sense of identity; and the implications for them when things go wrong.

SLIDE 9 — Identity and attachment

- The seven steps of infant attachment

– Claiming	Core identity
– Attunement	Stress regulation
– Affective attunement	Feelings and empathy
IDENTIFICATION	
– Impulse regulation	Morality
– Shame regulation	Social learning
– Rage management	Social acceptability
DIFFERENTIATION	
– Pre-cognitive patterning	Thinking
INTEGRATION	

These are the seven stages by which babies become attached to their carers. They are completely dependent on others for their very survival. This dependence, as they grow, develops into attachment relationships which turn them into responsive individuals who can regulate their own needs and impulses, manage their anger, live as part of the community and have satisfying reciprocal relationships with others.

What happens to the child during the earliest weeks, months and years – in particular his interactions with his caregivers – shapes the way his brain develops and has a profound effect on every aspect of his development. His experiences of attachment determine the very processes by which he is then able to think about anything else from then on.

Research evidence shows differences in structure and function between the brains of people of all ages who have experienced childhood trauma and those who have grown in a more secure and nurturing environment. More information on this subject can be found in the training materials produced by The Child Trauma Academy (see bibliography).

Claiming: this is the first stage in attachment, in which the key attachment figures in the birth community recognise the newborn baby as their own and take responsibility for caring for him.

Question: Can you think of any circumstances in which this might not happen?

Attunement is the mutual and reciprocal relationship which develops as a carer and baby learn more about each other's responses, and their bodies and brains, feelings and thoughts begin to work in tune with each other. The baby feels stress when she is hot, cold, uncomfortable or frightened. She cries. This is a sound which makes the carer feel stressed and uncomfortable, so he or she responds by meeting the baby's need and soothing her. As the carer feeds or soothes the baby, the carer's breathing slows down and his or her muscles relax and the baby follows suit. Because of the attention of the carer, the baby learns that stress is followed by soothing and relaxing. She learns to trust that her needs will be met. This is the foundation of being able to trust other people.

The baby will smile, coo and gurgle at the carer and this gives the carer pleasure so he or she responds to her; the carer's smiles, voice and attention are rewarding, so she does it some more.

Affective attunement develops when the baby tunes in to the carer's feelings and emotions. The baby will feel stressed when the carer is stressed, and she will become distressed if she sees the carer distressed. This is the start of being able to identify with other people.

Impulse regulation: we all have to learn to control our impulses if we are to be able to live in harmony with other people and obey societal rules. But young children need to be able to do this before they are able to think logically about rules or to understand why running into the road or pushing another child over is a bad idea.

Young children learn to control impulses through the feeling of shame. The feeling of shame works to keep them safe even before they have developed the capacity to think logically about the consequences of their actions.

This is how it works: when a toddler does something that could be dangerous to himself or someone else, an attuned carer reacts immediately to stop him doing it. The carer's reaction temporarily breaks the attunement between the child and carer. The child, often visibly shocked by this sudden change in the relationship, experiences shame and stops what he is doing. Toddlers who are constantly trying things out have to be "patterned" through shame to regulate their own impulses.

For the securely attached toddler, attunement is quickly re-established. When he controls his impulses, he is quickly rewarded by the reinstatement of the usual warmth and positive attention from the carer. This attunement–shame–reattunement cycle is called "re-integrative shame".

Of course, this process depends on attunement: an attuned carer will notice what the child is doing and react appropriately; the attuned child responds to this reaction by feeling shame. If attunement is lacking in the first place, neither of these things may happen.

Some experts believe that this process of impulse control through shame starts at around nine months and continues for about nine months. By 18 months the brain is developed enough for the child to be able to feel and think about social behaviour, social discipline and self-discipline.

Rage management: as the child develops, he gains a sense of himself as being separate from others. He realises that the world beyond himself can be the source of unpleasant feelings such as frustration, shame and fear. This can make him want to lash out and destroy whatever is producing the unpleasant feelings.

Question: Think about a child who has had a tantrum or rage when you were looking after him. Can you identify the feeling that triggered it in the child?

Young children can experience a powerful sense of rage in relation to something that seems small to us.

Rage comes from the limbic part of the brain called the amygdala, which is involved in the production of basic survival instincts. In adults, the limbic brain is usually kept "under control" by the activity of the cortex, which is the "thinking" brain. We consider the situation and decide on the response we want to make. But in young children, the cortex is still developing. Young children do not have the connections between the cortex and the limbic system which would allow them to transmit inhibitory signals and restrain the activity of the amygdala.

Most children are helped to manage and later to inhibit their own rage as a result of interaction with secure attachment figures. This helps to pattern the pathways in the brain to ensure that anger can be inhibited by the cortex.

This rage, this impulse to destroy, is the most powerful of the impulses that need to be regulated. Children who are unable to manage stress or control their impulses will not be able to manage their rage either. To other people, they may come across as volatile, unpredictable, threatening and even violent.

Differentiation: in the first year of life, the baby has no sense of herself as a separate identity from her caregivers.

Pre-cognitive patterning: in the first year, the baby cannot yet process her feelings or "think", but pre-cognitive patterning does take place. Repeated cycles build certain patterns in her brain – perhaps a sense of safety, a repeated sense of stress relieved by soothing and relaxation, the difference between night and day, how best to gain "control" of caregivers so that they will respond to her needs, and so on. These patterns will affect how the child can think later on in the development process.

During years 2–6, the cortex, or "thinking" brain, is developing. This allows abstract thought, and the functioning of this part of the brain will determine many of the individual attributes which make up the growing personality: creativity, abstract reasoning, humour, verbal competence, artistic flair and so on.

SLIDE 10   Attachment, identification and differentiation

- Claiming, attunement and affective attunement establish brain patterns allowing healthy identification
- Regulation of impulse, shame and rage establish brain patterns allowing differentiation
- Pre-cognitive patterning establishes underpinning structures to allow integration of the opposing forces, producing a spiral of development (Beck and Cowan, 1996, and Wilber, 2000)
- By the end of the infant attachment period, children have, or lack, patterns of brain function that allow flexible processes of identification, differentiation and integration
- On this basis, throughout life, humans build identity

We have seen how babies and young children learn, through attachment, both to identify with others and to differentiate from them. These two opposing forces are integrated as the child's brain function gradually develops and he has a growing sense of himself as being similar to others in some ways but also different and unique. This is his sense of identity.

SLIDE 11   Disruptions and distortions

- At each step of the developmental process linked to attachment, disruption or distortion has an enduring effect on identity
- Attachment relationships affect the structure of the developing brain
- Children with unmet attachment needs may be thinking and feeling with a different brain
- What sense do they make of their lives?
- Who do they think they are?

Whether basic feelings like trust and empathy develop depend on the quality of the attachment relationship between the baby and the caregiver. Where the caregiver is not responsive to the baby's needs, does not reliably soothe him and is not attuned to him, the right patterns are not laid down. Instead, the baby may remain in a continuously stressed state, feeling uncomfortable, afraid or unhappy over a prolonged period (known as "hyperarousal"), or he may dissociate or cut off from these feelings as a kind of protective mechanism.

Either way, the stress remains and the continued production of stress hormones has a damaging effect on the developing brain.

The effects of this can be far-reaching and long-lasting, impacting on every aspect of the way the child functions. It can affect the way he thinks, feels and behaves for years to come.

The next slides look in more detail at how unmet attachment needs can manifest themselves in the child's development and sense of identity.

SLIDE 12   Unmet needs for claiming

- Children who have not been able to claim and be claimed may be unable to form a core identity
- They have no basic foundation on which to build a personal sense of self
- They may be profoundly puzzled by relationships, and be unable to commit themselves to the necessary early step of identification with others
- Their core assumptions about themselves, the world and other people may be impaired or distorted

At this slide describes, claiming, the first stage in the attachment process, in which the key attachment figures in the birth community recognise the newborn baby as their own and take responsibility for caring for him, is fundamental for the baby to start to build a sense of self. If this need has not been met, the implications for the child's later sense of self can be severe.

SLIDE 13   Identity and core assumptions

- There are three core assumptions essential for good mental health (Janoff-Bulman, 1992):
- That the world is benevolent
  - "All shall be well . . ."
- That the world is meaningful
  - Humans are meaning-making animals
- That we are worthy
  - An accurate sense of entitlement
- These core assumptions are the basis for a secure sense of identity

Ronnie Janoff-Bulman (1992) came up with a model for thinking about the impact that trauma has on our ability to think. She considers that human beings are able to maintain good mental health by having three basic assumptions about the world: that the world is good and kind, that our lives have meaning, and that we are worthy or deserving. These assumptions are a way by which we explain the world to ourselves – patterns of thinking that are even more deep-seated than beliefs. They originate in babyhood, when our brains are forming in response to the way we are nurtured by our parents or other attachment figures.

These assumptions, of course, have no basis in fact. Our life experience often shows us that they are not the case – yet without these assumptions, we cannot function effectively.

Traumatic experience shatters these assumptions or prevents them from forming in the first place.

SLIDE 14   Unmet needs for attunement

- Children may be unable to regulate stress
- Day-to-day life may produce overwhelming stress leading to trauma
- Such traumatic stress closes down key areas of brain function, short-circuiting the rational brain
- This destroys core assumptions, or prevents the child from forming such assumptions
- Impairments or distortions in trust, the making of meaning, and appropriate entitlement damage the formation and maintenance of identity

SLIDE 15 Unmet needs for affective attunement

- The child may have difficulty with recognising and understanding feelings in self or others
- They may find no joy in social interaction
- They cannot generate a narrative that includes feelings
- They cannot take pleasure in joining in the production of a shared narrative
- They may therefore be impaired in their ability to form identity through identifying with others

A narrative is the story we tell ourselves (and sometimes others) about our lives. With our families, we have a shared history. We enjoy helping our children construct a narrative, when they ask questions like: 'Tell me about what happened when I was born' or 'When did I learn to read?'; or we talk about important events: 'Remember how sad we all felt when Granddad died?'

But children who never managed to have an attuned relationship with their caregivers when they were babies may have little sense of their own feelings and emotions, let alone those of others. They cannot experience empathy. They cannot imagine the inner experience of other people, so how can they ever identify with others?

Attunement, when a carer and baby learn to tune in to each other's needs, and affective attunement, when a baby learns to tune in to a carer's feelings and emotions, are vital steps in helping the baby to recognise her feelings, and those of others.

SLIDE 16 Unmet needs for regulation of impulse, shame and rage

- The child may be unable to manage destructive impulses
- They may be unable to account for their actions – moral accountability
- They may be subject to overwhelming shame in everyday situations
- Unregulated impulse, shame and rage may create a powerful negative sense of identity
- Unregulated shame may also impair or distort the key processes of identification and differentiation

As we have seen, most children learn to regulate their behaviour through reintegrative shame, in which their feelings of shame are quickly relieved as they are accepted back into the warmth of the attachment relationship.

But for some children, shame is not a transitory feeling. Without a secure attachment relationship, shame may be generalised and excessive, and children establish shame as part of their core identity. Instead of: 'I have done a shameful thing', they have the sense that: 'I am a shameful person'. This distortion happens before the brain is capable of processing emotions or forming conscious thoughts, so it is pervasive and deep-rooted.

Rage is a common response to the feeling of shame, and children who experience this kind of overwhelming shame are often controlling of others and chronically angry. Others may be compliant and feel worthless.

Some young children are made to feel ashamed by the adults around them when they express some other emotion such as distress, fear or rage. This creates a link between the particular emotion and shame, so that throughout life the child feels shame instead of the original emotion. In some people, shame substitutes for a drive such as sexuality or hunger.

Some children have also been "programmed" to feel shame whenever they express a basic need, such as the need to identify with or to differentiate from others. This can distort these processes which are so important in forming a sense of identity.

SLIDE 17   Unmet needs for pre-cognitive patterning

- **The child may have difficulty in thinking about and making sense of the world until they have developed through secure attachments such pre-cognitive patterns as:**
  - **Internal calendar and clock**
  - **Degrees of intimacy in relationships**
  - **Cause and effect**
  - **Fact and fantasy**
  - **Mine and yours**
- **They may be unable to differentiate themselves accurately and appropriately from others and the world around them**

Pre-cognitive patterning – the way in which repeated cycles build patterns in a baby's developing brain even before she is able to process her feelings or "think" – is an essential early stage in making sense of the world, and enabling the child to differentiate herself from others.

SLIDE 18   Impairments and distortions in the process of identification

- **These may occur if children:**
  - **Identify with people who harm them**
  - **Receive negative messages about people with whom they identify**
  - **Receive negative messages about gender, ethnicity, "race", culture, sexuality, sexual orientation, disability and so on**
  - **Are forced to identify with others against their will**
  - **Are prevented from identifying with others**
  - **Are unable to identify with others**

Exercise: Impairments and distortions in the process of identification

Ask the participants to divide into small groups of four and five. Give participants 15 minutes to complete the following exercise.

Display Slide 18 on the overhead projector. Ask participants, in discussion with others in their group, to come up with examples for each of the points on the slide.

Here are some examples.

- A child might identify with the older sibling who abused them.

- A child placed with a foster family might receive negative messages from members of that family about birth relatives with whom they identify.

- A child living in, say, Somalia or Sudan, who is abducted from his family and made to become a soldier is forced to identify with others against his will.

> - A child who is prevented from going to school or mixing with other children is unable to identify with his peers.
>
> Participants may be able to speak from experience about children they know, or know of. If not, they can use their wider knowledge or imagination to suggest situations in which these various impairments and distortions might occur.
>
> Ask each group to share one or two examples with the larger group.

SLIDE 19   **Impairments and distortions in the process of differentiation**

- **These may occur if children:**
  - **Receive negative messages about themselves as individuals**
  - **Are shamed if they try to differentiate themselves from attachment figures or key groups**
  - **Receive negative message about difference in relation to:**
    - **gender, ethnicity, "race", culture, sexuality, sexual orientation, disability and so on**

Being able to differentiate in a healthy way means being able to feel different or even hostile and yet still feel safe.

Here are examples of situations in which that might be difficult.

- Imagine a high-achieving child placed with a foster family where the other children are doing less well at school ('You think you're so clever . . .')

- Any self-respecting teenager wants to express her individuality somehow, whether it's by having multiple piercings or painting her bedroom black. There will be times when she is rude, hostile and dismissive of her parents' values. Some families will be able to tolerate this differentiation and continue to love and accept their teenager as she is. Others will feel threatened and try to force their son or daughter to conform to their own norms. (This can be a particularly difficult issue in some immigrant families, where cultures clash and the second generation have very different ideas and aspirations from those of their parents.)

Exercise: Impairments and distortions in the process of differentiation

Display Slide 19 on the overhead projector.

As in the exercise above, ask participants – in their small groups – to suggest other examples of situations in which these impairments and distortions might occur.

Ask each group to share one or two examples with the larger group.

End this session by inviting the participants to reflect on the foster carer's dilemma in the adolescent years – you may see a few wry smiles of recognition.

Adolescent to parents: 'I hate you.'

Adolescent to adoptive parents: 'I hate you and you're not my mum.'

Adolescent to foster carers: 'I hate you and you're not my mum and I'm telling my social worker.'

The next session will look at positive ways to help resolve these impairments, distortions and dilemmas.

1 Identity and child development

Enabling traumatised children to form a strong sense of identity and to celebrate diversity

SLIDE 20 **Enabling traumatised children to form a strong sense of identity and to celebrate diversity**

This slide introduces Session B.

In the first session, we learnt about how our sense of self is formed by identity and differentiation, and about how this process begins in early childhood. In this session, we will look at how traumatised children can be helped to form a strong sense of identity, even if this early process has not happened, or has been distorted.

SLIDE 21 **Trauma and identity**

- Traumatic stress disrupts key cognitive structures
- Even people with a well established sense of identity may be unable to maintain or recover positive self-constructs after developmental or emotional trauma
- Instead they develop a sense of self-as-helpless-victim, or self-as-helpless-perpetrator, or both
- Such core distortion is called traumatic identity
- Traumatic identity is often very persistent, long after the trauma has passed, and is resistant to change

We saw in Session A how unmet attachment needs in infancy – **developmental trauma** – can seriously impact on a child's growing sense of identity.

Trauma in later childhood or even adulthood – **emotional trauma** – can have a similarly damaging effect.

When a child who is securely attached suffers a horrific or terrifying event or a longer period of extreme fear or anxiety, it can have far-reaching effects on their brain and on many different aspects of their feelings and behaviour.

Even adults who have a well-established sense of identity may lose this if they suffer traumatic stress or a terrible shock, such as being in a terrible accident or witnessing the death of someone they love. Think about soldiers returning from battle with post-traumatic stress syndrome, for example.

When someone has suffered trauma, their whole outlook on life can change. They may begin to see themselves differently – as a helpless victim, for example. They develop beliefs such as: 'I am the sort of person to whom bad things happen' and 'I don't deserve anything good to happen to me'.

This new traumatic identity can persist for a long time.

SLIDE 22   Promoting secure attachment

- Carers can help children to begin to form a strong sense of identity through offering substitute primary attachment relationships
- Such relationships will recreate, in age-appropriate ways, the seven steps of the attachment process
  - Claiming – accepting and feeling accepted
  - Attunement – identification
  - Affective attunement – child responds emotionally to carer, takes notice of feelings of carer, discovers empathy and joy
  - Impulse, rage and shame – differentiation
  - Pre-cognitive patterning – through stability and order child gains the ability to think, to process and to make sense of identity

Carers can help to repair some of the damage caused when a child did not develop secure attachment relationships in babyhood. If you are aware of the seven stages of attachment, you can attempt to re-create the conditions for them to occur in ways that are appropriate for the child's age. This allows the child to begin to form a strong sense of identity at last.

The next few slides and exercises will encourage participants to think in more detail about this recovery process.

SLIDE 23   Claiming and attunement

- In order to be able to recreate the process of secure attachment, the child needs to be able to identify with the primary carers
- Think about the impact of diversity issues on this recovery process
  - How do issues such as gender, ethnicity, culture, "race", sexuality, disability and so on affect the process of identification with primary attachment figures?
- Discuss your thoughts within your group
- What are the key points arising from your discussion?

Exercise: Diversity

Ask participants to divide into small groups. Give them 10 minutes to complete this exercise.

Identifying with attachment figures is key to forming a sense of identity. This exercise invites participants to reflect on the way diversity issues could impact on this process.

Display Slide 23, and ask participants to discuss the questions on the slide.

Afterwards, ask one member of each group to share the key points with the group as a whole.

1

SLIDE 24   A child in mind: identification with others

- Think of a traumatised child or young person known to you for whom you think there are issues of diversity that have a negative impact on identification with primary attachment figures
    - What do you think the issues are for this child now?
    - What do you think the issues might be in the future?
    - What can be done to reduce harm and help the child to form a strong sense of identity?
- Discuss your thoughts within your group
- What are the key points arising from your discussion?

Exercise: Diversity and identification

Identifying with primary attachment figures, for instance, could be difficult for a child who is placed with a foster family in a transracial or transcultural placement. In their small groups, ask participants to think of a child or young person known to them who finds it difficult to identify with their primary attachment figures and to discuss the points on Slide 24.

Afterwards, ask one member of each group to share the key points with the group as a whole.

SLIDE 25   Differentiation from others

- In order to recreate the process of secure attachment, children need to be able to differentiate themselves from their environment and from their primary carers
- This differentiation enables them to develop an identity that can tolerate and celebrate diversity
- Differentiation occurs within a social milieu
    - Family, care setting, school, community, wider society
- Society, or particular social groups, may be institutionally oppressive or discriminatory in relation to any or all diversity issues

---

Being able to differentiate from others, safely, is vital in forming a sense of identity. We compare ourselves with others in our family, school, community and wider society. In any of these settings, we may be subject to discrimination and oppression in relation to our gender, ethnicity, culture, "race", sexuality, disability, age and so on.

SLIDE 26   Diversity and differentiation

- Think of a traumatised child or young person known to you for whom you think there are issues of diversity that have a negative impact on differentiation from primary attachment figures
    - What do you think the issues are for this child now?
    - What do you think the issues might be in the future?
    - What can be done to reduce harm and help the child to form a strong sense of identity?
- Discuss your thoughts within your group
- What are the key points arising from your discussion?

Children may not be able to differentiate in a healthy way from their birth family in order to fit into a new foster family. An example: imagine the difficulties facing a child of mixed heritage whose white birth mother was racist, if that child was placed in a black or mixed family.

Exercise: Diversity and differentiation

In their small groups, ask participants to think of a child or young person who has difficulties with differentiation and to discuss the questions on Slide 26. Ask one member of each small group to share the key points with the group as a whole.

SLIDE 27   Pre-cognitive patterning

- Children whose ability to create narrative has been impaired or distorted as a result of developmental or emotional trauma cannot form a strong sense of identity
- If they can form new secure attachment relationships, they can then begin to develop new underpinning patterns for thinking and feeling
- They can begin to develop an autobiographic self, and a personal narrative of identity
- Even if such recovery is impossible or limited, they can be helped to adapt and think in new ways
- Life story work is the key to recovery and adaptation

To have a strong sense of identity, you need to be able to tell yourself – and others – the story of your life. For the child who missed out in babyhood, a new secure attachment with a carer can be the start of being able to do this. Life story work, both formal and informal, builds on it.

One aspect of pre-cognitive patterning is developing a pattern for levels of intimacy in relationships. Children who failed to develop secure attachments may never have developed an understanding of appropriate levels of intimacy. If children lack this, carers can help them to adapt and work around their difficulties.

Most children have some intuitive understanding of relationships but the child who did not develop this early on needs his carer to explain to him that he has problems in this area and should take special care. At a basic level, the carer can teach him about what is appropriate by equipping him with some kind of structure or checklist to safeguard him from harm.

The aim is to get the child to stop and think: 'I have only just met this person – is it OK to go home with them?' or 'This person wants to kiss me – but they have said it has to be a secret. I remember my foster mum told me that means it's not OK.'

SLIDE 28   Developing selfhood

- Young children form a sense of self as they interact with their social world
- Attachment figures act as a living mirror, reflecting the child as loved/hated, accepted/rejected, respected/despised
- Every interaction provides the child with an image of self as perceived by others
- This interaction with primary attachment figures shapes and structures the growing brain
- It creates the basis for narrative and social accountability (Shotter, 1984)

The repeated interactions babies have with their attachment figures, both positive and negative, set up connections and patterns in their growing brain, shaping the way they feel about themselves and others. This is the basis for the child's personality and sense of identity.

Whenever the carer smiles at the baby or speaks lovingly, the baby takes from it a message: 'I am loved', or, at the very least, 'I can make people smile'.

SLIDE 29   Informal life story work

- Professional awareness applied to everyday interactions can help children to recover from impairments and distortions in the narrative process
- Day-to-day activities and events can be explored:
  - What happened?
  - What sense does the child make of that?
  - If there is impairment, how can we help the child to make sense of their experience?
  - If there is distortion, how can we help the child to reframe the experience constructively?
- This is informal life story work, and builds identity

Life story work is about enabling children to make sense of their lives and everything that has happened to them. Informal life story work is something that foster carers do every day, often without thinking of it as such.

On a daily basis, foster carers help the children in their care to manage school, friendships and out-of-school activities; where appropriate, they help them come to terms with their past and maintain contact with important people; they support them through life's frustrations and disappointments, celebrate their successes and build their self-esteem and independence.

Exercise: Informal life story work role-play

If time allows and participants are willing, you could include this role-play exercise. Ask one participant to play the child and another to play the adult – or, if there are no volunteers, do it yourself with your co-trainer!

The role-play illustrates how a carer might explore a particular event with a child. Day-to-day events like these are an opportunity for informal life story work and for building a positive sense of identity in the child.

Here are some scenarios you could choose from, or you may have ideas of your own.

1. Robert, aged eight, has got into trouble for misbehaving at school. He comes in from school, throws his bag on the floor and shouts: 'My teacher hates me! Everyone hates me!'

2. You have been fostering 10-year-old Andreas for six months. Today he is refusing to go to school. There is going to be a lesson about drug addiction and his birth father is a drug addict.

3. Five-year-old Chanelle is in her room, crying and saying that no one likes her. She has always had difficulty interacting with other children because she is subject to unpredictable outbursts of anger, although she does have two friends. Her two friends have been invited to a party but she hasn't been invited.

4. 14-year-old Louis, who has no contact with his birth family, has been watching a soap opera in which a character meets his long-lost birth mother. He goes uncharacteristically quiet.

5. 15-year-old Sally is in the Girl Guides. She enjoys it but she is thinking of leaving because the other girls in her class are more interested in nightclubs and they are making fun of her for being a Guide.

SLIDE 30   Formal life story work

- **Sometimes children need to work with adults to produce a formal account of their own history**
- **Such work may be needed if, for example:**
  - **Children are separated from primary attachment figures**
  - **Vulnerable children are facing a transition**
  - **There are specific diversity issues affecting the ability of the child to form a strong identity**
- **Formal life story work is time limited**
- **There is a product: a book, memory box, CD, DVD . . .**
- **It will be repeated and updated throughout childhood**
- **Both process and product value and contain identity for, and with, the child**

Most children's life stories are held in the collective memory of their parents, siblings and extended family, in the photos that fill the family albums and the home videos on the shelves, and the boxes of mementoes and keepsakes – the first pair of shoes, the first painting, the swimming certificates. For children separated from their families, who may go through many partings and moves, there is a need for someone to take on the work of recording the child's life story.

Usually the person who does formal life story work is a social worker or therapist. Both the time spent sitting down and talking with the child about it, and the product itself, are important. It fills in some gaps, tells the child about significant events and people in her life, and helps her understand why she has turned into the person she is.

NB The second training course in this programme, *Life story work: enabling children to make sense of their lives*, deals with life story work in more detail, so you may wish to invite participants to attend this next course if your agency is planning to run it.

SLIDE 31 ## Resilience and identity

- **The ability to survive and thrive under difficult conditions**
  - **Resilient people continue to develop to their own potential even when circumstances are against them**
- **Different from coping**
  - **Survive but at cost to own healthy development**
- **Individual and social factors contribute**
- **A strong sense of identity enhances resilience**
- **Resilience enhances a strong sense of identity**

Resilience is not the same as coping. When we "cope" with difficulties or changes in our life we survive them, but at a cost, for instance, we may use alcohol as a crutch, avoid certain situations or vent our feelings on others in inappropriate ways. When we are resilient, we find ways of dealing with difficulties that allow us to continue to develop to our full potential.

Factors at the individual level that affect resilience include the child's own personal strengths, skills and attributes. Social factors include support from others in the child's network, including foster carers, teachers and other school staff, social workers, therapists and leaders of activity groups or religious communities.

A strong sense of identity will enhance a child's resilience. Resilience will also enhance a strong sense of identity. So, for traumatised children, promoting their resilience can also help to develop their selfhood and self-esteem.

SLIDE 32 ## The six domains of resilience in childhood

- **Factors increasing resilience can be organised into six domains (Daniel and Wassell, 2002a, b and c)**
  - **Secure base**
  - **Education**
  - **Friendships**
  - **Talents and interests**
  - **Positive values**
  - **Social competencies**
- **Secure attachment is the most stable and reliable foundation for resilience in all domains**

A child can be more or less resilient in these various domains. For instance, he may be doing very well at school but have few friendships. Or he may be struggling academically but be socially very competent and excel in talents and interests outside school.

SLIDE 33   Identification with others

- Who are the key people who constitute the first layers of the support network for the child or young person you have been thinking about?
  - Foster carers or residential staff?
  - Family members?
  - Friends?
  - School staff?
  - Social worker?
  - Therapist?
  - Community activity leaders?
  - Religious community leaders?
- With whom does this child identify?

Ask participants to recall one of the children or young people they considered during one of the earlier exercises. Now ask them to make a note of significant people in the child's life and consider which of them the child identifies with.

SLIDE 34   Promoting resilience

- What impact do each of the key network members have in each domain?
  - Secure base
  - Education
  - Friendships
  - Talents and interests
  - Positive values
  - Social competencies
- What will enable them to promote resilience effectively for this child or young person?
- How can the child and carers engage these key people in the work of promoting resilience?

Exercise: Promoting resilience

Ask participants to divide into small groups. Give them 15 minutes to complete this exercise.

The exercise builds on the notes participants will have just made about a child and significant people in that child's life.

Slide 34 asks participants to look in detail about how the significant people affect each domain. It also asks them to consider how to alert these people to the part they could play in encouraging the child's resilience. Participants should discuss these questions in their groups.

The unique individual and their heritage

- Make a note of some ways in which the child or young person you have in mind is unique, special or different
- Are there diversity issues which make this child different from significant attachment figures?
- Is the child able to regulate issues of shame?
- Discuss your thoughts with others around you
- What are the key points from your discussion?

Exercise: The unique individual

Give participants 15 minutes to complete this exercise.

What are the child's special interests and skills? What gives her most delight? What makes people warm to her? What difficulties has she overcome? What makes her different from other children of her age?

Remind participants of what they learned in the earlier session about unmet attachment needs and the regulation of shame: the way pervasive shame can become part of a child's identity and the way children may come to experience shame as a substitute for other emotions and drives.

Ask participants, in small groups, to discuss the questions on this slide. Afterwards, ask one member of each group to feed back key points to the group as a whole.

SLIDE 36 **Celebrating diversity**

- Make a plan to work with the child or young person you have in mind on developing their ability to value their individuality and to tolerate and celebrate diversity
  - Who? Who else? How? Where? By when?
- One achievable step, not the whole journey
- Discuss your plan with others around you
- What are the key points arising from your discussion?

Exercise: Helping a child to value their individuality and celebrate diversity

Give participants 15 minutes to complete this exercise.

Slide 36 asks for positive, practical ideas for carers and others to encourage the child to feel proud of himself and the things that make him different from others around him.

Other adults from the community, such as neighbours, teachers and leaders of activity groups and cultural and religious groups the child belongs to, could also be enlisted here. What could they do to encourage the child's self-esteem?

For instance, in the case of a child who needs support to feel proud of his ethnicity:

● Foster carers could find out if there are any local community groups for people from the child's country of origin. They could take him there to meet new friends of his own age; they could go with him to cultural and social events that celebrate his heritage.

● A friend or neighbour from the same country of origin and ethnicity as the child could teach him to cook a traditional meal from their country or play a traditional instrument.

● A teacher could ask the child to put together a special project about his country of origin to share with the rest of the class.

Ask participants to share their ideas with their small group and then discuss these with the larger group. You might want to write these ideas and suggestions on the flipchart; later, you could transcribe them and distribute the list to participants after the course, to act as a reminder.

SLIDE 37   In conclusion

● **To build a strong sense of identity children must be able to identify with others, to differentiate from others, and to integrate the two into one narrative**
  – **Secure attachment underpins these processes**
  – **Developmental and emotional trauma disrupt and distort the formation of identity**
  – **Diversity issues may have a destructive impact**
● **Traumatic identity is persistent**
  – **Work on identity with traumatised children is long term and slow, with some moments of illumination**
● **Resilient adults who celebrate diversity can enable traumatised children to build strong identity**

This sums up the content of the two sessions. Working together with others, carers can do a great deal to help the children in their care to grow up with a strong and positive sense of identity.

SLIDE 38   Implications for practice

● **Please take some time to complete the evaluation form in your pack**
● **We need your comments on the course and how you will use it in your practice**
● **If you would like more information on Akamas courses, visit www.akamas.co.uk**

An evaluation form is available on the CD-ROM.

2 Life story work

Child development and the creation of narrative

This is the first session of the second course in this book, **Life story work**, so welcome the participants and put them at their ease.

For any participants who did not attend the previous course – **Identity and child development** – explain what they can expect: that there will be some direct input from you, in terms of your slide presentation, but that they will also have a lot to contribute from their own knowledge and experience. Explain that they will not simply be sitting and listening to you – they will be actively involved in discussion and group exercises, coming up with their own thoughts, ideas and suggestions.

Introductions

If any participants are new to the group and did not attend earlier sessions, ask them to introduce themselves to the rest of the group.

Ground rules

You may want to reiterate the ground rules that were set out at the start of Session A in the first course.

Provide the handout

Give participants a handout of the slide presentation so that they do not need to write everything down – they can make additional notes on their handout if this is helpful.

SLIDE 1   Life story work: enabling children to make sense of their lives

However great the adversity they have survived, traumatised children need to know the story of their lives. This allows them to access and deal with their feelings and to develop a positive sense of identity.

SLIDE 2   Learning outcomes

- **To understand how children develop a personal narrative**
- **To understand the effect of trauma on this narrative**
- **To consider how trauma affects children's sense of identity**
- **To understand how formal and informal life story work helps children to make sense of their lives**

This slide shows the learning outcomes for Session A, *Child development and the creation of narrative*, and Session B, *Enabling traumatised children to form a strong and positive personal narrative*.

SLIDE 3 Child development and the creation of narrative

This slide introduces Session A of the course.

SLIDE 4 About personal narrative

- As humans beings we do not just live our lives, we tell ourselves the story of the life we are living
  > 'The first trick behind consciousness is the creation of this account, and its first result is the feeling of knowing. Knowing springs to life in the story.' (Damasio, 1999, p 172)

The difference between humans and animals is that, as humans, we are conscious of our own existence. We "know" we are alive; we can reflect on our past and anticipate our future.

SLIDE 5 The beginning of narrative

- Babies do not have a sense of who they are
- As in everything, they are dependent for this on their carers
- Every interaction is a message to the baby
- For example – baby smiles – carer smiles
  - The message could be:
    - I am loved
    - I am attractive to others
    - I can make people smile

At birth, babies do not have a sense of themselves as a separate person. They are not aware of themselves as someone separate from their carers. This awareness begins to develop in the first months of life.

It is shaped by the baby's interactions with his caregiver. The nature of these interactions shapes the baby's sense of who he is. This is why the quality of the baby's attachment relationships are so crucial to his sense of identity and his developing personality. Is he loved, valued, listened to? Do his caregivers notice and respond to his needs? Do they delight in his company, do they take pleasure in making him smile and laugh? Or is he ignored – or worse?

SLIDES 6 to 12 Identity and attachment

- The seven steps of infant attachment

– Claiming	– core identity
– Attunement	– trust
– Affective attunement	– feelings and empathy
– Impulse regulation	– morality
– Shame regulation	– social learning
– Rage management	– social acceptability
– Pre-cognitive patterning	– thinking

Disruptions and distortions

- At each step of the developmental process linked to attachment, disruption or distortion has an enduring effect on identity
- Attachment relationships affect the structure of the developing brain
- Children with unmet attachment needs may be thinking and feeling with a different brain
- What sense do they make of their lives?

Unmet needs for claiming

- Children may be unable to form a core identity
- They may be profoundly puzzled by relationships
- They may lack any fundamental sense of safety
- They have no basic foundation on which to build a personal narrative

Unmet needs for attunement

- Children may be unable to regulate stress
- They may be unable to form secure trust relationships
- Day-to-day life may produce overwhelming stress leading to trauma
- Such trauma affects the ability to create language and meaning
- The capacity to produce narrative is impaired

Unmet needs for affective attunement

- The child may have difficulty with recognising and understanding feelings in self or others
- They may find no joy in social interaction
- They cannot generate a narrative that includes feelings
- They cannot take pleasure in joining in the production of a shared narrative

Unmet needs for regulation of impulse, shame and rage

- The child may be unable to manage destructive impulses
- They may be unable to account for their actions – moral accountability
- They may be subject to overwhelming shame in everyday situations
- They will be unable to produce an accurate and balanced personal narrative

Unmet needs for pre-cognitive patterning

- The child may have difficulty in thinking about and making sense of the world until they have developed through secure attachments such pre-cognitive patterns as:
  - Internal calendar and clock
  - Degrees of intimacy in relationships
  - Cause and effect
  - Fact and fantasy

This section comprises a number of slides on **identity and attachment**, and possible effects of **disruptions and distortions** in the attachment process. This section is included in the first course in this book, **Identity and child development**.

- If participants have already completed the **Identity and child development** course, simply run through the slides in this section quickly as a reminder, noting in each case the implications of unmet attachment needs for the child's ability to create a personal narrative.

- If you are running this course, **Life story work**, as a stand-alone course, please refer back to **Identity and child development** for background information on these slides (see Slide 9, *Identity and attachment* through to Slide 17, *Unmet needs for pre-cognitive patterning*, earlier in this book).

SLIDE 13   Trauma and identity

- **Traumatic stress disrupts key cognitive structures**
- **Even people with a well established sense of identity may be unable to maintain or recover positive self-constructs after developmental or emotional trauma**
- **Instead they develop a sense of self-as-helpless-victim – traumatic identity**
- **This traumatic identity may be persistent**

We have seen how unmet attachment needs in infancy – **developmental trauma** – can seriously impact on a child's growing sense of identity.

Trauma in later childhood or even adulthood – **emotional trauma** – can have a similarly damaging effect. It can have far-reaching effects on the brain and on many different aspects of the person's feelings and behaviour.

When someone has suffered trauma, their sense of identity can change. They may see themselves as a victim, as someone who is powerless, unlucky or cursed.

SLIDE 14   The seven dimensions of child development

- **Research from the Looking After Children System showed seven dimensions of development important to parents:**
  - **Identity**
  - **Family and social relationships**
  - **Emotional and behavioural development**
  - **Social presentation**
  - **Education**
  - **Health**
  - **Self-care skills**
- **Narrative work should address each of these dimensions**

In the 1990s, the Department of Health produced the Looking After Children system, based on research into the milestones that most parents look for to reassure themselves that their child is thriving. The research led to a system for monitoring outcomes for children looked after in the care system.

Anyone working with children on their life stories should consider each of these dimensions. The next set of slides asks participants to consider the importance of each dimension in turn and the effect of impairments and distortions on this particular aspect of the child's development.

SLIDE 15   Identity

- We form a sense of who we are in two ways:
  - We identify ourselves as similar to others
  - We identify ourselves as different from others
- Make a list of all the people or groups with whom you identify yourself
- Make a list of all the things about yourself that make you feel unique, special or different
- Discuss your lists with people in your group and make a note of any key points arising from your discussion

---

Exercise: Identifying with others

This exercise appears in the first course, **Identity and child development** (Slides 5 and 6). So if participants have also been on the **Identity and child development** course, omit this exercise.

SLIDE 16   Impairments and distortions in the identity narrative

- These may occur if children:
  - Identify with people who harm them
  - Receive negative messages about people with whom they identify
  - Receive negative message about gender, ethnicity, "race", culture, sexuality, sexual orientation, disability
  - Are forced to identify with others against their will
  - Are prevented from identifying with others
  - Are uanble to identify with others
  - Are given negative messages about themselves

Impairments and distortions in a child's identity narrative might occur, for instance, if:

- a child identified with the older sibling who abused them;
- a child placed with a foster family received negative messages from members of that family about birth relatives with whom they identify;
- a child was prevented from going to school or mixing with other children, and so was unable to identify with her peers.

Participants may be able to think of other examples from experience of other children they know, or know of.

●●●●●●●●●●

SLIDE 17   **Family and social relationships**

- If you were writing the story of your life, which relationships would first come to mind as shaping the person you are?
  - When did the relationship begin?
  - How long did it last?
  - What is the quality of the relationship?
  - How has it affected your life?
- Discuss your findings with people within your group and make a note of any key points

---

Exercise: Influential relationships

Divide participants into small groups. Give them 15 minutes to complete this exercise.

Slide 17 asks participants to reflect on relationships that have influenced them, at any stage of their life. Some relationships will have been positive; others, such as those with bullying work colleagues or abusive partners, may have been painful or unpleasant at the time but experiencing them may have made the individual stronger or more insightful, for instance.

Ask participants to discuss the questions on the slide in their small groups.

 Question: If you could meet up again with any person from your childhood, who would it be – and why?

●●●●●●●●●●

SLIDE 18   **Impairments and distortions in the relationship narrative**

- The personal narrative may be impaired, so that children have no concept of certain kinds of relationships
- It may be distorted, so that children have mistaken beliefs, such as:
  - People who love me will always abuse me
  - Men and women hurt one another
  - Adults can't be trusted
  - Other children dislike me

Children who have been neglected or abused have missed out on being "parented" and developing trust, and may have little or no experience of a protective, nurturing relationship.

Traumatised children are in "survival mode" so the pleasures of sociability mean nothing to them. They may pay little attention to other people – instead of enjoying the company or friendship of others, they see them as resources to be used, or as a means to an end.

 Question: Have you ever cared for a child like this? What was it like to try to establish a relationship with this child?

SLIDE 19 Emotional and behavioural development

- Secure attachment creates links between feelings, thoughts and actions
- This allows personal, social and moral accountability
  - Who we are
  - How we feel
  - Why we behave as we do
- Children with unmet attachment needs may be unable to produce such accounts
- Traumatic stress changes brain function and may diminish such accountability

This is about emotional literacy. To function well as a social being, it is necessary to understand feelings (starting with our own).

Question: Have you ever had the experience of asking a child why they have done a particular thing, for instance, trashed their room or torn up their homework, and meeting with a completely blank response?

Some children literally have no idea why they behave as they do. They have never learned to interpret their own feelings and cannot link feelings with behaviour.

SLIDE 20 Impairments and distortions in the emotional and behavioural narrative

- Impairments may include:
  - Being unable to express feelings through language
  - Being cut off from emotional experience
  - Lack of impulse regulation
  - Inability to think about own behaviour and make sense of it
  - Lack of shame regulation
- Distortions may include:
  - Inability to express some feelings in words
  - Shame-binds, shame replacing banned feelings
  - Blaming others for their own feelings
  - Taking responsibility for how others feel
  - Magical thinking

Traumatised children find it difficult to construct narrative and meaning. They often experience emotional numbness and lose the capacity for joy in living. Children who struggle with impulse, shame and rage can end up in trouble because of problematic behaviours such as stealing, lying, destructiveness, violence and aggression. Other people find the child bewildering and unpredictable.

Self-harm may be another way of "acting out" the emotions they do not feel or cannot express.

They may try to ease their stress through unusual, compulsive or obsessive behaviours. "Magical thinking" is a distortion in which the child believes that she has the power to control things and events which are actually outside her control: 'If I stay in my room and don't go to school, my mum won't die'.

SLIDE 21   Social presentation

- Secure attachment enables social survival
  - Self-confidence
  - Sensitivity to others
  - Awareness of rules and norms
  - Ability to judge the limits of social acceptability
  - Adaptability in different situations
  - Autonomy in relation to adherence to social norms
- Unmet needs can leave children unable to fit in with or adapt to social expectations

Children who are securely attached develop an understanding of how to behave in social situations and present themselves in a way that is acceptable to other people. They understand that they are expected to do as the teacher says, for example. Children who have been traumatised are not so fortunate – they may come across as odd or uncomfortable to be around. They are unable to experience empathy or express their emotions appropriately and are subject to a different set of taboos and social inhibitions from their peers. Their overwhelming sense of shame may lead to the need to be in control in a social situation; or it may mean they resist any environment or relationship which provides them with positive messages.

Most children love to be praised, but for children with unmet attachment needs, it can be too overwhelming to cope with.

'I can't bear it when I get praised in my review meeting,' said one young man. 'I usually have to break stuff afterwards.'

 Question: Have you ever cared for a child who found it difficult, even painful, to be praised or complimented? How did this show itself in his or her behaviour?

SLIDE 22   Impairments and distortions in the social presentation narrative

- Think of a traumatised child or young person known to you
- Make a list of any indicators that there may be impairments or distortions in relation to the social presentation narrative for them
  - Does this child or young person find it difficult to make any sense of how they appear to other people?
  - Or do they have a distorted view of how they appear to others?
  - If the child you think of shows no such indicators – think of another child!

Exercise: Impairments and distortions in the social presentation narrative

Divide participants into small groups. Give them 15 minutes to complete this exercise.

Most participants will be able to think of a particular traumatised child or young person who does not "fit in" socially, does not seem to understand how they come across to others, or who is "thick-skinned" and doesn't pick up on the usual social cues.

Ask them to list examples of the ways this manifests itself in the child or young person's day-to-day life. Afterwards, ask them to share their thoughts with others in their small group.

SLIDE 23

Education

- **Think of one message that you were given about yourself as a child in relation to education**
  - **Who gave you the message?**
  - **What was the effect on you as a child?**
  - **What has been the effect on you as an adult?**
- **What people believe about themselves in relation to education has a powerful effect on their ability to learn and to achieve educational success**

Allow participants a couple of minutes to think about this. Afterwards, one or two of them may want to share their memories and insights with the group as a whole.

SLIDE 24

Impairments and distortions in the education narrative

- **Many traumatised children struggle with education**
- **They may receive negative messages from carers, school staff, or their peers**
- **They may misunderstand positive messages**
- **They may be unable to form a narrative, and therefore be unable to think about education at all**
- **They may have distorted beliefs about themselves and education**

Children who have been traumatised are likely to be impaired in their ability to learn and to remember. They are also likely to have difficulties with socially-based learning which involves co-operating in groups, and with learning that depends on understanding the inner world of others, such as literature. Other problems will stem from their own self-image, forged from the messages they have received from other people ('You are too stupid to be able to do this'; 'No one from our family was ever any good at school').

SLIDE 25   Health

- There are two aspects to the creation of a health narrative
- The story of our genetic history
    - General health of family members
    - Longevity
    - Specific inherited conditions
    - Beliefs about who we "take after"
- Our beliefs and attitudes in relation to our own health
    - Messages acquired in childhood about health in general
    - Childhood messages about our own health

SLIDE 26   Impairments and distortions in the health narrative

- Many traumatised children are impaired in their ability to create a narrative, and therefore cannot think about their own health
- They may have very little information on which to base an accurate narrative about their family health history
- They may have distorted beliefs about themselves and health
- It is important to make no assumptions about what children understand or believe about their own health

Question: Have you ever been surprised by something a child says or believes about their health? How do you think they formed this belief?

SLIDE 27   Self-care

- From the beginning of narrative formation in young children, issues of dependence, independence and interdependence are part of the story
- The nature of this story the child tells themselves affects every aspect of self-care
- Healthy development is a gradual move from dependency on reliable adults towards autonomy and mutual care
- This produces a narrative of competence that enables children to believe in their ability to function as adults

SLIDE 28   Impairments and distortions in the self-care narrative

- Children and young people in whom the self-care narrative is impaired will be unable to think about becoming adult
  - They may switch off or panic when there is any discussion about growing up
  - They may develop very disturbed behaviour in later adolescence
- Distortions in the self-care narrative produce distorted thinking about their own adult life
  - They may overestimate their ability to live without adult help
  - They may have an exaggerated fantasy of adult life
  - They may show infantile "magical thinking" instead of age-appropriate planning

Question: Have you ever cared for a child or young person who was clingy and over-dependent? Have you ever cared for one who fiercely refused all adult help even when he clearly needed it?

SLIDE 29   Informal life story work

- Informal life story work uses awareness of narrative formation to help children recover and adapt after adversity
  - Narrative formation is continuous – we are always building our life story – every event feeds into the narrative
  - Impairments and distortions lead to misreading of events
  - Informal life story work enables children to discover and build a new narrative through everyday experience
    - What happened?
    - What does the child think happened?
  - All significant adults contribute to informal life story work
  - Teamwork is essential

As we have seen, most children in foster care or residential care will have received some distorted or negative messages about themselves during the formative period of early development. Foster carers and other significant adults can work towards helping children overcome the effects of harmful messages they have received. They can try to ensure the child receives enough accurate and positive messages to form a strong and positive personal narrative. They can do this as part of everyday life at home and school.

SLIDE 30   Formal life story work

- Traumatised children have an impaired or distorted life narrative
  - Trauma causes impairments and distortions
  - They may also be separated from their family and have little or inaccurate information
  - Their family as a whole may function with an impaired or distorted narrative
- Formal life story work is an essential service to traumatised children
  - It provides a mechanism to discover and store accurate information
  - It enables children to link facts, feelings and memories
  - It takes place at key points to build on informal work

When children are separated from their birth family, there will be times when they need to take part in a formal process of life story work. Usually it is someone outside the foster family who takes on the task of life story work with the child. This person will study files and records, visit people and places and use various techniques to help the child develop and understand their life story. They will put together a collection of physical reminders of the child's life, and at the same time they help him access the memories and feelings that went along with his experiences.

The next session will look in more detail at informal and formal life story work.

2 Life story work

Enabling traumatised children to form a strong and positive personal narrative

SLIDE 31 **Enabling traumatised children to form a strong and positive personal narrative**

This slide introduces Session B.

In the first session, we learnt about how a baby's sense of self and personal narrative can be distorted by trauma.

To develop a strong and positive personal narrative, children need to be able to build resources of memory about times when they have felt happy, or strong, or have survived against the odds. They also need to remember the hurtful and sometimes harmful experiences they have lived through – these are just as much a part of their life story. Bringing these memories to mind may also bring back the feelings they felt at the time. And children with unmet attachment needs or who have suffered traumatic stress often find it difficult to express or deal with feelings. Workers with the right skills can help them to do this.

There is a continuous line linking life story work and therapy. At one end of that line is the gathering and recording of known facts for the child to keep. At the other is intensive psychotherapy to enable the child to address and integrate traumatic life events. Somewhere in the middle of that line, life story work stops and therapy begins.

SLIDE 32 **Day-to-day narrative work**

- Think of a traumatised child or young person known to you
- Imagine an average day in their life
- Think of one occasion when there is interaction between the child and their carer
- What message do you think the child received and built into their life story as a result of this interaction?
  - Think about the narrative the child forms in each developmental dimension
- Can you imagine a child who would receive the *opposite* message from the same interaction?

Exercise: Day-to-day narrative work

Display Slide 32 on the overhead projector.

Ask participants to complete this exercise alone – if any of them are having difficulty, they could discuss it with a partner.

This exercise reminds participants of what they learned in Session A, **Child development and the creation of narrative**, about how children form narrative and self-image based on their interactions with their carers. Every interaction between carer and child is being built into the child's life story. This will happen whether we are aware of it or not.

SLIDE 33 Using informal life story work

- The message given or intended and the message received may be very different, for example:
  - A hug = I am loved
  - A hug = I am not loved (love = hitting)
  - A hug = I am sexually desired
- Adults can only guess what message the child receives from any interaction
- We need to check our guesses, but not so often as to become intrusive
- We need to make our *intentions* explicit and clear

Because children who are fostered are often subject to cognitive impairments and distortions, we need to do everything we can to ensure that the intentions behind all our actions are clear and not misinterpreted.

SLIDE 34 Formal life story work and the review system

- When children are separated from their families, it is particularly important that they have access to formal life story work when this is needed
- The review system is a mechanism to ensure that the child's needs for life story work are recognised and met
- The need for formal life story work to be undertaken or updated should be considered at every review of the care plan for the child
- When the need for such work is identified the work should be included in the care plan

Most children's life story is held safely for them by their family, with whom they have a shared history. Separated children, by definition, do not have day-to-day access to their birth family and the source of their own life story. So it is the responsibility of those in the care system to ensure that children do have a record of the truths about their lives and what has happened to them.

Life story work should be done during arranged meetings with the most appropriate person for the child and it should happen in various age-appropriate ways throughout her childhood.

SLIDE 35   Informal and formal life story work

- Who should undertake the work?
  - Informal work is best done by those in close daily contact with the child
  - Formal work is best done by people outside the child's daily life who have access to records and have skills in life story work
  - Who is the most appropriate person to work with this child at this stage of development? Issues to consider include:
    - Age and gender of child and worker
    - Ethnicity, culture, "race", religion
    - Disability and communication issues

SLIDE 36   Linking informal and formal life story work

- Preparation for formal life story work
  - What needs to be done to prepare for formal life story work?
  - What should be included in the book, box, etc?
- Dealing with feelings
  - Techniques and methods for helping children to access and deal with feelings
- The impact of formal life story work
  - The process is likely to have an impact on the child and on everyone around the child
  - Formal life story work planning needs to include thinking about the impact on the whole network

Formal life story work is not just about collecting names, dates and photographs. Life stories are as much about feelings as about facts.

 Question: Can you suggest some of the methods that might be used in formal life story work to help a child to understand her story and to access and deal with her feelings?

Possible techniques and methods for life story work include:

- Timelines
- Flowcharts
- Family trees
- Charts showing important people in the child's life
- Maps showing important places
- Using computers
- Using telephones
- Using puppets
- Playing games
- Playing with toys
- Drawing faces for feelings
- Using poetry
- Telling stories
- Drama
- Groupwork

Question: Have you ever looked after a child while formal life story work was going on? How, and how much, were you involved?

●●●●●●●●●●
SLIDE 37   **Thinking about the impact of such work**

- In turn, think about the impact of formal life story work on each of the following:
  - The child
  - The carers
  - The sons and daughters of carers
  - The child's family
- What general conclusions could you draw about the likely impact of life story work on the child and the network around the child?
- What can be done to ensure that each child gets the most benefit from life story work?

Exercise: The impact of life story work

Ask participants, in small groups, to consider and discuss the questions on Slide 37. Afterwards, ask one person from each group to share some of their conclusions with the group as a whole.

The carer

However much they might want to help, carers cannot be therapists for the child – either the caring or the therapy would be destroyed. Can the carer accept this?

- Life story work involves contact with members of the child's birth family, which does not usually fit well with the role of the carer.
- Carers can sometimes do formal life story work but that decision should be made by the team with careful thought and the work must be well supervised.
- As a general rule, carers can certainly undertake some aspects of life story work, such as taking the child to visit significant places. How might this impact on their own children?
- Whoever carries out the life story work, it is the carers – and their own children – who have to deal on a day-to-day basis with any emotional and/or behavioural fall-out after the child or young person's life story work session.

Members of the child's birth family are crucial to life story work. They need to be appropriately involved and to contribute as much as possible to the process. However, this may evoke painful memories and possibly feelings of guilt for them.

SLIDE 38   The need for teamwork

- Both informal and formal life story work require that the adults work as a team
- Informal work is happening through every interaction between an adult and a child
  - What are the messages this child is receiving?
  - What sense do they make of these messages?
- Formal life story work needs meticulous planning agreed with all significant adults, including:
  - Roles and responsibilities
  - Methods and techniques
  - Dealing with feelings
  - Supporting the child and supporting the network

Life story work must address all the experiences that make up the child's life. Whether informal or formal life story work, helping a child to understand a life that has included neglect, abuse or trauma is demanding and challenging for carers and social workers. They need expert training and support.

Teamwork is also vital because different people may be involved in different aspects of formal life story work.

People undertaking formal life story work need the knowledge to judge when the child needs therapy rather than life story work – and the resources must be there for therapy when it is needed.

SLIDE 39   Implications for practice

- Please take some time to complete the evaluation form in your pack
- We need your comments on the course and how you will use it in your practice
- If you would like more information on Akamas courses, visit www.akamas.co.uk

An evaluation form is available on the CD-ROM.

3 Family ties

The complexity of sibling relationships

This is the first session of the third course in this book, **Family ties**, so welcome the participants and put them at their ease.

For any participants who did not attend the previous course – **Life story work** – explain what they can expect: that there will be some direct input from you, in terms of your slide presentation, but that they will also have a lot to contribute from their own knowledge and experience. Explain that they will not simply be sitting and listening to you – they will be actively involved in discussion and group exercises, coming up with their own thoughts, ideas and suggestions.

Introductions

If any participants are new to the group and did not attend earlier sessions, ask them to introduce themselves to the rest of the group.

Ground rules

You may want to reiterate the ground rules that were set out at the start of Session A in the first course.

Provide the handout

Give participants a handout of the slide presentation so that they do not need to write everything down – they can make additional notes on their handout if this is helpful.

SLIDE 1 **Family ties: working with issues in the care of siblings**

Remind participants about building resilience and the importance of close and intimate relationships with family and friends.

Growing up with brothers and sisters can enhance the sense of a secure base and shared values in childhood; it can mean company, friendship, fun, support and solidarity and a rich arena for learning to get along with others.

But sibling relationships can also go badly wrong and result in negative and destructive experiences. Anyone with responsibility for a traumatised child must pay careful attention to that child's experience of the sibling relationship. It is vital to carry out careful assessment so that you recognise and minimise any risks associated with the relationship, and recognise and promote any benefits. Sibling relationships change over time, so these assessments need to be reviewed and updated throughout childhood.

SLIDE 2 Learning outcomes

- To consider the variety of sibling and sibling-type relationships
- To consider the lifetime implications of separation from siblings
- To understand the planning and assessment process
- To consider issues of contact between separated siblings

This slide sets out the learning outcomes for Session A, *The complexity of sibling relationships*, and Session B, *Assessment and planning*.

SLIDE 3 The complexity of sibling relationships

This slide introduces Session A of this course.

SLIDE 4 Who is my sibling?

- Do you have anyone you think of as a sibling?
- What is their biological relationship to you?
  - Do you have two parents in common?
  - Do you have one parent in common?
  - Is there some other bond of kinship between you?
- What do your answers indicate about kinship patterns in your culture?
- Discuss with others and note key points

Exercise: Who is my sibling?

Display Slide 4 on the overhead projector. Divide participants into small groups to discuss the questions on the slide. Give them 10 minutes to complete this exercise.

The questions on Slide 4 may well illustrate that there is no simple definition of a sibling. There may be participants who have grown up with a cousin or even a niece or nephew close to them in age, with whom they developed a sibling-type relationship. Some actual sibling relationships may not be close, particularly if the siblings were brought up in separate households.

●●●●●●●●●●
SLIDE 5   **Some definitions**

- Kosonen (1996)
    - Children who share at least one parent
    - Children who have lived in the same household as each other
    - Children who would have lived together had they not been received into care
- Children/adults with one or more of the following:
    - common genes
    - common history, family values, culture
    - common legal status

In the past there have been instances in which twins, genetically identical but separated at birth, not only did not meet but were not even aware of each other's existence.

At the other extreme, children who do not share any genetic material but who are brought up in the same family may consider themselves siblings. Adopted children share neither genes nor a common history with their new brothers and sisters in their adoptive family, but their legal status is the same.

●●●●●●●●●●
SLIDE 6   **What do children think?**

> The loss of a sibling in childhood is a traumatic event which continues to be felt in adulthood with pain and feelings of isolation. For those who stay with their siblings after separation from their parents, the relationship may act as a protective factor in terms of their feelings of identity, security and self worth. (Barbara Prynn, 2001)

●●●●●●●●●●
SLIDE 7   **Benefits and drawbacks**

- What do you think are the benefits of sibling relationships:
    - In childhood?
    - Over a lifetime?
- What do you think are the drawbacks?
- Discuss your ideas with other people and make a note of any key points

---

Exercise: Benefits and drawbacks of sibling relationships

Display Slide 7 on the overhead projector. Give participants 10 minutes to complete this exercise.

Ask participants, in small groups, to discuss the questions on the slide. Prompt them to consider dysfunctional families, stressful environments and children in the care system as well as normal family life. Afterwards, ask one member of each group to feed back to the larger group.

SLIDE 8   The benefits of sibling relationships

- High emotional quality – uninhibited, individualised, intimate
- Familiarity – shared experiences, home, adults, peers, community, play, learning, shared narrative
- Contribution to each other's development
- Close long-term attachments
- Learning to be part of a social group, group dynamics and social development
- Protection against negative environment
- Shared support in stress and developing resilience
- Learning about responsibility for others
- Longest relationships over a lifetime

This and the following slide list some of the points that may have emerged during the previous exercise.

SLIDE 9   The drawbacks of sibling relationships

- Rivalry and conflict
- Exploitation
- Hierarchy and power issues
- Continuing dysfunctional patterns of behaviour
- Incompatible needs – development and recovery
  - Developmental delay leading to competing needs
  - Triggering destructive memories of trauma
  - Dominant child blocking recovery process for others
- Loyalty issues – birth family/carers

SLIDE 10   Specific issues

- Think about the effects of specific issues of oppression or discrimination on sibling relationships
  - The impact of such issues as gender, culture, ethnicity, class and disability on:
    - Relationships between siblings
    - Siblings separated from their family
    - Siblings separated from each other
    - Siblings placed with other children
- Discuss your ideas with other people and make a note of any key points

Issues of oppression and discrimination have implications for sibling relationships too. For example, consider the issues for the children in the following scenarios:

- Identical twins: one twin was brain-damaged through lack of oxygen at birth, the other is perfectly healthy.

- A brother and sister, whose mother is white, have different fathers, one of whom was black and the other white. The children are placed together with foster carers; their foster mother is white and their foster father is black.

- Two sisters aged eight and 12, from a family of travellers, are placed together in a middle-class foster family. The family lives in a middle-class area and their birth children attend a "good" school close to home.

- A girl is brought up with four younger brothers and a father who believes firmly that it is her place to help her mother around the house.

Exercise: Specific issues and sibling relationships

Display Slide 10, and ask participants, in small groups, to discuss the issues on the slide. Give participants 15 minutes to complete this exercise.

Afterwards, ask one member of each group to feed back to the larger group.

SLIDE 11   **Lifetime implications**

- **Separated siblings may lose:**
  - **A lifelong relationship**
  - **Support in adversity**
  - **A shared history**
  - **Sense of kinship**
  - **Continuity and rootedness**
  - **Sources of knowledge about family**
  - **Resources for identity building**

Our longest lifetime relationships are usually with our brothers and sisters. It is not only at the time of separation that siblings suffer a loss. They miss out on forming a close bond and sharing their childhood years, but there are also implications for the rest of their lives, at times when they might otherwise have been there for each other.

SLIDE 12   **What do separated siblings think?**

- **Thoughts about separation depend upon:**
  - **Child's definition of a sibling**
  - **Previous separations**
  - **Significance within families of patterns of attachment, support, care giving**
  - **The child's sense of the quality of the relationships**
  - **Role of the individual child in the family – "the meaning of the child"**
  - **Power dynamics: oppression and support**
- **Children can be more optimistic and positive regarding siblings than the adults around them**

Question: Have you ever cared for a child who was separated from his or her siblings? How did he or she feel about it?

SLIDE 13   The guiding principle

- Children should be placed together with their siblings unless there are exceptional circumstances

SLIDE 14   Exceptional circumstances

- Dysfunctional and destructive patterns of interaction
    - Themes of rivalry or exploitation often based on gender
    - Chronic scapegoating
    - Maintaining unhelpful alliances or conflicts from family of origin
    - Maintaining unhelpful hierarchical positions
    - Incompatible recovery needs – unmanageable together
    - Highly sexualised behaviour between siblings
    - Siblings triggering each other's traumatic material (Smith, 1998)

Where these harmful patterns of interaction have been identified, professionals may decide it is best to place siblings separately. The next session looks in more detail at the assessment process.

3 Family ties

Assessment and planning

In the first session, we learnt about the benefits and drawbacks of sibling relationships, and the lifelong implications of keeping siblings together or apart.

How should professionals go about making these complex and crucial decisions?

SLIDE 15   Assessment and planning

This slide introduces Session B of the course.

SLIDE 16   The context of assessment of need

- **Family of origin – culture, ethnicity, unique structure**
- **Pattern of particular sibling relationships over time**
- **Impact of number of siblings, ages, gender, impairments, and so on**
- **Sibling relationships are uninhibited emotionally**
  - **Such uninhibited relationships may be victimising, abusive or exploitative**
  - **They may also be very close and supportive**
- **Each sibling has their own individual coping mechanisms and their own resilience**
- **Safety issues must be considered for each child**

Every situation is unique; as is each individual child, and each sibling relationship. All of the factors on Slide 16 must be taken into account when making decisions about the care of siblings.

SLIDE 17   Factors influencing sibling relationships

- **Quality of parent–child relationship and early attachment**
- **Quality of parental relationship – conflict/stress/abuse**
- **Emotional climate in the family as a whole**
- **Impact of abuse on abused and non-abused members of family – may lead to hostility between siblings**
- **Child's perception of how parents treated self and siblings**
- **Impact of non-shared environment between siblings**
- **Age and gender of each child**
- **Child's views on sibling relationships – general and particular**

SLIDE 18 Factors to consider in assessment

- Family environment (emotional climate)
- Each child's relationship with parent
- Quality of parenting
- Input of parent(s) and others to sibling relationship
- Expectation of child's role
- Environmental stresses
- Extended family input to care
- Temperament of each child
- Birth order/age gaps/gender

SLIDE 19 Assessing sibling relationships

- Gathering perceptions
  - Child's own view – often differs from adult's
  - Carers'/birth family's perception – social work assessment
  - Earlier experiences
    - How much experience did these siblings share?
    - Quality of parenting experienced by each child
  - Current environment
    - Carers' attitude – opportunities for contact – degree to which carers promote sibling relationships – other children in living group
  - Observations from other environments
    - School, family centre, leisure activities, etc
    - Extended family

When assessing sibling relationships, it is important that views are sought from a wide range of people connected with the children, as well as from the carers and the children themselves. This enables a fuller and more representative picture of the sibling relationship in different environments and over time to be obtained.

Question: Have you ever looked after siblings? Was there any question of separating them and, if so, did a social worker seek your views on the relationship?

SLIDE 20   Gathering evidence

- Individual and sibling group flow charts
- Seeing siblings both together and separately
- Dyads and small group relationships
- Observation of group without adult interaction
- Identifying particular sibling roles
- Individual temperaments
- Birth experiences and order, gender, "race", disability issues
- Range and frequency of sibling behaviour shown
- Setting behaviour in context – past/present
- Potential for change in any dysfunctional patterns

As well as people's perceptions and opinions, the person carrying out the assessment needs to look at evidence from the siblings' behaviour and, if there are damaging patterns of behaviour, assess the potential for these to change.

SLIDE 21   Obtaining the views of those who know the children well

- Family
- Wider kin network
- Carers
- Previous carers
- School
- Medical professionals
- Significant others

SLIDE 22   Decision-making – Kay Donley, 1983

- Examine importance of sibling relationship – now and throughout life
- Consider child's feelings – part of the decision making process
- Decisions made by several people – those with knowledge
- Document all reasons for and against
- If separated, make plans for contact

It is important that such an important decision as separating siblings is not made by one professional alone. The reasons for and against separation need to be weighed up – this is not a decision to make on instinct alone. The reasons must be recorded, in case anyone needs to know them later on.

SLIDE 23   Children in mind

- Work with others to create a living case study of children about whom professionals need to make plans to support a sibling placement
    - What are the key issues in the planning process?
        - The needs of each child
        - The needs of the birth family
        - The needs of the care family
    - Who are the key people who should be involved in the planning process?
- Using ideas discussed today, note any new possibilities that come to mind. How can these be brought into the planning process for the children?

Exercise: Planning to support a sibling placement

Display Slide 23 on the overhead projector. Divide participants into small groups to consider the questions on the slide. Give them 15 minutes to complete this exercise.

Ask participants to think of actual children – if they do not know of any in this situation at the moment, they may think of children they have known in the past. If there are some participants who cannot think of any children in this situation, ask them to pair up with someone who can.

This exercise asks participants to think about the planning that is needed for siblings to be placed together.

If siblings are to be separated, there should be some plans for contact between them – this is the subject of a later exercise (Slide 30).

The next few slides look at the issue of contact between separated siblings.

SLIDE 24   Contact between siblings: lifetime patterns in sibling relationships

- Lifetime patterns can be very different in different cultures
- Many siblings are separated as children
- Siblings usually live separately as adults
- Siblings may support one another at many different life stages
- Separated siblings may search for and find one another

SLIDE 25

The benefits of contact for siblings separated in childhood

- Continuity
- Reduced anxiety
- Support
- Increased awareness of family culture and identity
- Shared positive memories
- Appreciation of developmental progress
- Contributing to recovery from trauma of each child
- Shared life story work

SLIDE 26

The drawbacks of contact for siblings separated in childhood

- Each child interferes with recovery of the other, triggering trauma
- Continuing or reinforcing patterns of abuse, exploitation or scapegoating
- Different contact arrangements with parents or significant others have negative impact
- Different placement experiences produce jealousy or conflict
- Siblings may inhibit each other's development

As we can see, there can be both benefits and drawbacks for siblings separated in childhood: of course, every situation, every child and every sibling relationship is unique.

SLIDE 27

Different forms of contact

- Face-to-face planned formal contact
- Face-to-face unplanned or casual contact
- Video conferences
- Telephone and text messaging
- Letters and cards
- Email
- Photographs
- Presents
- Anniversaries, birthdays, special events
- Shared rituals and ceremonies

Contact may be carefully planned and can take many forms, but in some situations real life can intervene and things can get messy. Children are often placed close to home, and separated siblings may meet up anywhere from in school to chance meetings on the street. Workers need to be aware of these possibilities when planning placements and contact.

SLIDE 28 Contact and life story work

- Separate individual life story work
- Shared life story work
- Each sibling contributing to the life story of the other
- Photographs, mementoes, video material
- Looking forward as well as looking back

The second course, **Life story work**, looked at the importance of this work in building the child's identity. Participants who attended the previous course will be familiar with the term "life story work". If not, you may need to explain.

In the case of siblings, life story work – or some of it, relating to their shared history – could be carried out with the children together.

SLIDE 29 Building for the future

- Preparing for a lifetime relationship
- What would each child hope for from the sibling group?
- What would each child most fear?
- How can the benefits of the sibling relationship be maximised?
- How can the drawbacks of the sibling relationship be minimised?

SLIDE 30 Children in mind

- Work with others to create a living case study of children about whom professionals need to make plans to support relationships in a separated sibling group
  - What are the key issues in the planning process?
  - Who are the key people who should be involved in the planning process?
- Using ideas discussed today, note any new possibilities that come to mind. How can these be brought into the planning process for the children?

Exercise: Planning with children in mind

Display Slide 30 on the overhead projector. Divide participants into small groups to consider the questions on the slide. Give them 20 minutes to complete this exercise.

Again, ask participants to think of actual children. If there are some participants who cannot think of any children in this situation, ask them to pair up with someone who can.

This exercise asks participants to think about the issues of contact and life story work when planning for separated siblings.

SLIDE 31   To sum up

- Caring for brothers and sisters separated from their family is complex
- There is no simple definition of a sibling
- There is no simple way of assessing sibling groups
- Sibling relationships both persist and change over time
- It is the responsibility of every professional concerned with looked after siblings to ensure that risks associated with sibling relationships are assessed, minimised and managed
- It is also essential to ensure that present and future benefits of these relationships are promoted and maintained

Question: Now that you have considered sibling relationships in more depth, how will this affect the way you work?

SLIDE 32   Implications for practice

- Please take some time to complete the evaluation form in your pack
- We need your comments on the course and how you will use it in your practice
- If you would like more information on Akamas courses, visit www.akamas.co.uk

An evaluation form is available on the CD-ROM.

4 Contact

Understanding the complexity of contact

This is the first session of the fourth course in this book, **Contact**, so welcome the participants and put them at their ease.

For any participants who did not attend the previous course – **Family ties** – explain what they can expect: that there will be some direct input from you, in terms of your slide presentation, but that they will also have a lot to contribute from their own knowledge and experience. Explain that they will not simply be sitting and listening to you – they will be actively involved in discussion and group exercises, coming up with their own thoughts, ideas and suggestions.

Introductions

If any participants are new to the group and did not attend earlier sessions, ask them to introduce themselves to the rest of the group.

Ground rules

You may want to reiterate the ground rules that were set out at the start of Session A in the first course.

Provide the handout

Give participants a handout of the slide presentation so that they do not need to write everything down – they can make additional notes on their handout if this is helpful.

SLIDE 1 Contact: issues of identity and stability

For every child separated from her birth family, a decision has to be made about whether or not contact with birth relatives would be a good thing for the child. This course looks at how contact can affect a child's identity and stability.

SLIDE 2 Learning outcomes

- **To understand how to gather and weigh evidence when making contact decisions**
- **To understand how cultural differences can affect family ties**
- **To understand the effect of secondary traumatic stress on caregivers**
- **To understand how to assess and manage risk when making contact decisions**

This slide outlines the learning outcomes for Session A, *Understanding the complexity of contact*, and Session B, *Making child-centred contact plans*.

SLIDE 3   Understanding the complexity of contact

This slide introduces Session A of this course.

SLIDE 4   What is contact?

- Think of someone you care about that you might see soon
- How would you describe seeing them?
  - Going home?
  - Visiting?
  - Dropping in?
  - Meeting for coffee or a meal?
- Would you ever describe such a meeting as "having contact"?

The rhetorical questions on this slide challenge participants to think about what "having contact" means. In fostering terms, the concept of "contact" implies a legal, regulatory structure – but for a child in care, as for any of us, spending time with a person who is significant in your life is a very human process. Planning contact means imposing rules, agreements and limitations on this process.

SLIDE 5   Contact in caring for looked after children

- Contact is a means for a separated child to maintain a relationship with members of their birth family
- It makes it possible for the child to maintain and process attachment relationships formed in infancy

The child's birth parents may not be able to offer him security and stability but they are still significant to his sense of identity. There may be benefits in continued contact with attachment figures, provided that these benefits outweigh any perceived risk to the child.

SLIDE 6   Direct and indirect contact

- Direct contact:
  - Face-to-face meetings
  - Telephone calls
  - Messaging
  - Video conference meetings
- Indirect contact
  - Letters and cards
  - Audio and video tapes
  - Email

Question: In which circumstances do you think direct contact is best, and when do you think indirect contact might be necessary?

SLIDE 7   Case study

- A six-year-old girl with a care plan for permanent placement
  - Mother: drugs, alcohol, severe depression
  - Neglect, developmental delay
  - Originally removed from home two years ago
  - Care order contested: rehab and assessment
  - Physical abuse: broken arm – mother's partner?
  - Care order and plan for permanence

Ask participants to consider the case outlined on Slide 7, and to jot down the main points of information shown.

SLIDE 8   The case for and against

- Everyone to the left of the room jot down as many points as possible FOR maintaining face-to-face contact with her mother for this child
- Everyone to the right of the room jot down as many points as possible AGAINST maintaining face-to-face contact with her mother for this child
- Persuade the other group that you are right!

Exercise: The case for and against contact

Display Slide 8 on the overhead projector. You may need to return to displaying Slide 7, if requested by the participants. Give them 10 minutes to complete this exercise.

Decide how you would like to manage this exercise. You could put participants into small groups and get them to argue it out. Or perhaps you will have a free-for-all, no-holds-barred debate! Either way, it will quickly become clear that the issue of contact generates strong feelings. Once people have taken a view, they often begin to defend it passionately, even with so slight a case study. There is no research evidence that can give clear answers. Proper contact planning is always a matter of professional judgement in the presence of strong feelings.

SLIDE 9　Too much complexity, too little evidence

- Factors contributing to complexity include:
  - Age
    - At first separation
    - At subsequent separations
    - Now
  - Attachment relationships
  - History of unmet needs and traumatic experiences
  - Siblings
  - Cultural expectations
  - Effects of contact on care family

SLIDE 10　Age matters

- Each child has different needs at different stages of their development in relation to their birth family
- What sense does this child, at this stage of development, make of their life?
- Who matters to them? How do we know?
- What are the likely benefits of contact with members of their birth family?

The balance of risks and benefits to the child of having contact with birth relatives will vary at different ages and stages of development. That is why any contact decision must be monitored and reviewed over time.

SLIDES 11 to 17　Identity and attachment to Unmet needs for pre-cognitive patterning

- The seven steps of infant attachment
  - Claiming   Core identity
  - Attunement   Trust
  - Affective attunement   Feelings and empathy
  - Impulsive regulation   Morality
  - Shame regulation   Social learning
  - Rage management   Social acceptability
  - Pre-cognitive patterning   Thinking

Disruptions and distortions

- At each step of the developmental process linked to attachment, disruption or distortion has an enduring effect on identity
- Attachment relationships affect the structure of the developing brain
- Children with unmet attachment needs may be thinking and feeling with a different brain
- What sense do they make of their lives?

Unmet needs for claiming

- Children may be unable to form a core identity
- They may be profoundly puzzled by relationships
- They may lack any fundamental sense of safety
- Contact may be meaningless until the primary needs have been met

Unmet needs for attunement

- Children may be unable to regulate stress
- They may be unable to form secure trust relationships
- Contact may produce overwhelming stress leading to trauma until the child has developed key trust relationships that soothe the child and enable self-regulation

Unmet needs for affective attunement

- The child may have difficulty with recognising and understanding feelings in self or others
- They may find no joy in social interaction
- They may not be motivated for contact until, through secure attachments, they have developed emotional literacy and the capacity for joy in relating to others

Unmet needs for regulation of impulse, shame and rage

- The child may be unable to manage destructive impulses
- They may be unable to account for their actions
- Contact may provoke unmanageable impulses, or rage, or overwhelming shame until the child has developed self-regulation through secure attachment relationships

Unmet needs for pre-cognitive patterning

- The child may have difficulty in thinking about and making sense of contact until they have developed through secure attachments such pre-cognitive patterns as:
  - Degrees of intimacy in relationships
  - Cause and effect
  - Fact and fantasy

Contact is important for children to build a sense of their own identity.

This section comprises a number of slides on identity and attachment and possible effects of disruptions and distortions in the attachment process. This section is included in the first course, *Identity and child development* (Slides 9, 11, 12, 14, 15, 16 and 17) and links this to issues of contact. It is vital when planning contact to work out what sense the child makes of it, and what impact the contact is having on their further development. This structure helps carers to see how they can help children to get the most benefit from contact. It can also help the team to plan contact over time to fit with the child's recovery from trauma.

- If you are running **Contact: issues of identity and stability** as a stand-alone course, please refer back to **Identity and child development** for background information on these slides (*Identity and attachment* through to *Unmet needs for pre-cognitive patterning*, Slides 9, 11, 12, 14, 15, 16 and 17).

SLIDE 18   Trauma and identity

- Traumatic stress disrupts key cognitive structures
- Even people with a well established sense of identity may be unable to maintain or recover positive self-constructs after traumatic experience
- Instead they develop a sense of self-as-helpless-victim
- This traumatic identity may be persistent

We have seen how unmet attachment needs in infancy – **developmental trauma** – can seriously impact on a child's growing sense of identity.

Trauma in later childhood or even adulthood – **emotional trauma** – can have a similarly damaging effect. It can have far-reaching effects on the brain and on many different aspects of the person's feelings and behaviour. When someone has suffered trauma, their sense of identity can change. They may see themselves as a victim, as someone who is powerless, unlucky or cursed.

SLIDE 19   Trauma and contact

- For traumatised children, contact may trigger traumatic recall
  - They may be retraumatised
  - They may recover memories that enable them to process the trauma and recover
- Contact may increase traumatic identity
- But contact may also, at other times, resolve traumatic identity and allow the child to discover other possible identities

Contact for traumatised children does involve some degree of risk; but, perhaps surprisingly, in some cases it may also help them to recover. This is why it is essential to understand the issues and carefully weigh up the evidence before making decisions on contact.

SLIDE 20   Contact and siblings

- Attachment relationships are one-to-one
- Each sibling has different needs
- Each set of needs is dynamic
- Siblings can support and resolve contact issues for each other
- They can also cause each other heartache and distress

If participants have attended the previous course, **Family ties: working with issues in the care of siblings**, they will have already considered these issues in detail.

SLIDE 21   Contact and culture

- Discuss the following questions with people nearby:
- What contact do you have with members of your kinship group?
  - Who do you count as kin?
  - How much contact do you have?
  - What sort of contact?
- How do your answers to these questions relate to your cultural origins?

Exercise: Contact and culture

Display Slide 21 on the overhead projector. Give participants 10 minutes to complete this exercise.

Participants' responses to this exercise will probably illustrate wide variations between families in terms of how close family members are and how frequently they see each other. It may illustrate some cultural variations too – you may find that among Asian participants, for example, grandparents are more likely to live with the family group compared with families of British origin.

SLIDE 22   Culture and complexity

- The meanings ascribed to family and contact between family members are very different in different cultural settings
- These cultural differences add further complexity to thinking about contact between separated children and members of their birth family

People responsible for planning contact between children and their birth families must be aware of these cultural differences and take them into account in decision-making.

SLIDE 23   Contact and the care family

- Members of the care family form attachment relationships with the child
- Although formed after infancy, these may have the quality of infant attachment relationships because the child has unmet needs or has been traumatised
- Contact for the child with birth family members may provoke strong feelings in members of the care family

 Question: Have you ever looked after a child who had contact with birth relatives? How did you feel about the contact? Why do you think you felt like that?

SLIDE 24   Contact and secondary trauma

- **Members of the care family may experience secondary traumatic stress**
  - **Empathy produces physiological changes as though exposed to trauma**
  - **Brain function changes**
  - **People become less articulate, less emotionally literate, more angry or despairing**
- **Secondary trauma may lead to avoidance, resistance or sabotage**

Secondary traumatic stress is the stress that results from caring for or about someone who has been traumatised. People who are empathic and care for children who have been neglected or abused are vulnerable to developing secondary traumatic stress.

The signs and indicators include: anger, tearfulness, fearfulness; physiological arousal such as jumpiness, nightmares and hypervigilance; exhaustion; and changed sleeping and eating patterns. People suffering from secondary traumatic stress feel increasingly isolated and alienated, and their morale is low.

Avoidance of traumatic material – talking about difficult events or emotions, and any triggers that might remind us of them – is another understandable response to stress. Carers may be upset or angry about proposals for contact, stop communicating with other members of the team and be reluctant to co-operate with the plans.

The next session will look at how we can try to prevent such damaging situations from arising.

4 Contact

Making child-centred contact plans

In the first session, we looked at some of the issues to be considered when planning contact, and how contact can affect the identity of traumatised children. In this session, we look at making child-centred contact plans, including considering the risks that may be involved.

Being a parent involves constantly assessing and managing risks. When a child asks to go out and play, when a teenager wants to go to a party, we will usually ask questions: Who will she be with? Where will she be? How late is it? How will she get home? And so on. We think about the potential risks, asking ourselves what could go wrong. We also weigh up the benefits: how much she wants to go, how good it will be for her to get out of the house, how important it is in terms of her friendships, and so on. Then we weigh up the possible risks and benefits and come to a decision based on that particular situation – although, most of the time, we may not even consciously realise this is what we are doing.

The foster caring profession is somewhat different. Children in foster care are often traumatised and troubled children who show a range of difficult and challenging behaviours. As a result, as well as being subject to the normal risks of childhood and adolescence, these children and young people may face particular risks or present particular risks to others.

Social workers and foster carers are paid to make decisions for these children in a publicly accountable activity on behalf of the care system. The decisions they have to make are often complex and even life-changing. Therefore they need to go through a conscious process of assessing and managing risks and to be able to account for decisions they make.

Contact between a child and birth relatives is not without risk. For carers too, it brings involvement with people who may be unpredictable, angry and even aggressive.

SLIDE 25   Making child-centred contact plans

This slide introduces Session B.

SLIDE 26   The wishes and feelings of the child

- **Must be taken into account**
- **Unmet needs in relation to infant attachment and recovery from trauma may distort or impair a child's ability to make sense of family relationships**
  (Schofield, 1998)

Question: Have you ever looked after a child who has an unswerving sense of loyalty to the people who have harmed him, and an antipathy towards all those doing their best to care for and protect him?

SLIDE 27   Assessing and managing risk

- **What is the hazard?**
  - – Name each hazard for the child associated with contact
  - – Be very specific and clear
- **Assessing risk**
  - – What is the level of risk associated with each hazard?
  - – What factors affect the risk?
- **Minimising risk**
  - – Reducing vulnerability
  - – Providing protection
- **Balancing benefits against risks**
  - – What are the benefits?
  - – Do the benefits outweigh the risks?

If participants have been on the BAAF/Akamas training course *Safer Caring* (Cairns, 2007) they will have an understanding of risk in foster care. This slide asks them to look at risk in the context of planning contact.

- Name the hazard – vagueness leads to a generalised anxiety which is not helpful. Think about situation, duration and other factors. How do other key people feel about this hazard?

- Assess the level of risk: is it negligible, tolerable, moderate, substantial or intolerable?

These levels relate to the seriousness of the harm that could result from the hazard and the level of probability that the hazard will occur (see below). This is a tool used in the context of health and safety at work, to estimate the level of risk associated with workplace hazards such as toxic substances. But it can be adapted for use in the context of contact in foster care – where, of course, the hazards are less tangible and far more complex.

Level of harm	Slightly harmful	Harmful	Extremely harmful
Probability			
Highly unlikely	Negligible risk	Tolerable risk	Moderate risk
Unlikely	Tolerable risk	Moderate risk	Substantial risk
Likely	Moderate risk	Substantial risk	Intolerable risk

Minimising risk: there are two ways of doing this, by considering the level of harm that would occur from a hazard, and the probability that it would occur. In terms of protection strategies, **what** will be done by **whom** and **when** or under **what circumstances?**

Balancing benefits against risks: again, it is important to be clear about the benefits that are associated with a particular hazard. Obtain different views about the benefits and then form a judgment about whether the risks outweigh the benefits or *vice versa*.

SLIDE 28   Risk is inevitable and dynamic

- Risk is never zero
  - Assessments must indicate level of risk as low, medium or high
  - We work to manage, not eliminate, risk
- Risk is never static
  - Assessments indicate a level of risk at a certain time and place
  - Management must include monitoring and review

Life is unpredictable and it is never possible to eliminate risk altogether. All we can do is to attempt to keep risk at an acceptable level. To be meaningful, any risk assessment must indicate the level of risk.

Risk can change in response to many things. Risk management means keeping an eye on the level of risk and reviewing whether the current level of protection is enough.

In some situations where the decision is not to have any contact, there may still be a risk of the child or young person coming into contact with birth relatives in an unplanned way, for instance, meeting on the street or in shops, especially if they live in the same neighbourhood.

SLIDES 29 and 30   *A child in mind* and *Some points to consider*

- Think of a child or young person known to you who is separated from their family and in the care of the local authority
- Jot down key points that you think should be considered when making a contact plan for this child or young person
- Focus on the needs of the child

- What is the purpose of the contact?
  - In the short term?
  - In the long term?
- What are the benefits to the child?
- What are the risks to the child?
- What sense can the child make of it?
- What sense does the child make of it?
- Are the carers able and willing to support the contact plan?

Exercise: A child in mind

Display Slides 29 and 30 on the overhead projector. Give participants 15 minutes to complete this exercise.

Ask participants to get into small groups. Each person should think of a child or young person and address the questions on Slide 30.

Afterwards, ask for one volunteer from each group to briefly sum up the issues for their particular child.

SLIDE 31   Including risk management in planning

- Involve others, including the child
- Identify factors that reduce risk
- Identify factors that enhance benefits
- Identify appropriate strategies for protection
- Indicate WHAT will be done BY WHOM and WHEN and under WHAT CIRCUMSTANCES
- Indicate how the plan will be reviewed, and what changes would prompt early review
- Record the plan

Working as part of a team is essential. Different people may see a situation differently and perceive and respond to a risk differently. Some people in the care team may even be affected by secondary traumatic stress disorder and this will affect their views. So it is important to involve others.

There should be a risk management plan, with clarity about roles and lines of responsibility. There should be clear, open and frequent communication between all parties.

Agencies must ensure that practice and the way in which people work shows awareness of risk. All agencies need to have monitoring, review and evaluation policies.

SLIDE 32   There is no such thing as pain-free contact

- Affectional bonds change us
- Disrupting, distorting or breaking such bonds is painful
- Children separated from their attachment figures suffer loss whether or not they have contact with birth family members
- Care families deal with issues of attachment and trauma whether or not the child has contact with birth family members
- The welfare of the child is always paramount

Contact will never be pain-free for the child, but can still on balance be beneficial to her, including in the long term.

Adults emotionally involved with a child in care – whether birth relatives or carers – are likely to have strong feelings about contact and whether it should be allowed or not, how often and so on. The adults need to maintain perspective and remember that contact is not about them – it's about the child. It is about what the child needs, now and in the future.

 Question: Now that you understand more about contact, how will this affect the way you work?

SLIDE 33   Implications for practice

- Please take some time to complete the evaluation form in your pack
- We need your comments on the course and how you will use it in your practice
- If you would like more information on Akamas courses, visit www.akamas.co.uk

An evaluation form is available on the CD-ROM.

Bibliography

Beck D E and Cowan C C (1996) *Spiral Dynamics: Mastering values, leadership and change*, Bodmin: Blackwell Business

Cairns K (2007) *Safer Caring: A training programme*, London: BAAF

The Child Trauma Academy: see www.childtrauma.org and www.childtraumaacademy.org

Damasio A (1999) *The Feeling of What Happens: Body and emotion in the making of consciousness*, Orlando, FL: Harcourt

Daniel B and Wassell S (2002a) *Assessing and Promoting Resilience in Vulnerable Children: The early years* (volume 1), London: Jessica Kingsley

Daniel B and Wassell S (2002b) *Assessing and Promoting Resilience in Vulnerable Children: The school years* (volume 2), London: Jessica Kingsley

Daniel B and Wassell S (2002c) *Assessing and Promoting Resilience in Vulnerable Children: Adolescence* (volume 3), London: Jessica Kingsley

Donley K (1983) *Opening New Doors,* London: BAAF

Durkheim E (1997) *The Division of Labour in Society*, New York: The Free Press

Janoff-Bulman R (1992) *Shattered Assumptions: Towards a new psychology of trauma*, New York: The Free Press

Kosonen M (1996) 'Maintaining sibling relationships: neglected dimension in child care practice', *British Journal of Social Work*, 26, pp 809–822

Prynn Barbara (2001) 'Family building in adoption', *Adoption & Fostering*, 25:1, pp 33–43

Schofield G (1998) 'Making sense of the ascertainable wishes and feelings of insecurely attached children', *Child and Family Law Quarterly*, 10:4, pp 363–375

Shotter J (1984) *Social Accountability and Selfhood*, Oxford: Basil Blackwell

Wilber K (2000) *Integral Psychology: Consciousness, spirit, psychology, therapy*, Boston: Shambhala Publications